This Book Belongs to

Book 3

Content and Artwork by **Gooseberry Patch Company**

LEISURE ARTS
Vice President and Editor-at-Large: Anne Van Wagner Childs
Vice President and Editor-in-Chief: Sandra Graham Case
Director of Designer Relations: Debra Nettles
Publications Director: Kristine Anderson Mertes
Design Director: Cyndi Hansen
Editorial Director: Susan Frantz Wiles
Creative Art Director: Gloria Bearden
Photography Director: Karen Hall
Art Operations Director: Jeff Curtis
Licensed Product Coordinator: Lisa Truxton Curton

EDITORIAL STAFF

EDITORIAL
Managing Editors: Suzie Puckett and Linda L. Trimble
Senior Associate Editor: Jennifer L. Riley
Associate Editor: Susan McManus Johnson

TECHNICAL
Managing Editor: Theresa Hicks Young
Technical Writers: Sherry Solida Ford and Leslie Schick Gorrell
Knitting Editors: Lois J. Long and Linda Luder
Technical Associate: K.J. Smith

FOODS
Foods Editor: Jane Kenner Prather

OXMOOR HOUSE
Senior Editor: Susan Carlisle Payne
Editor: Kelly Hooper Troiano
Senior Photographer: Jim Bathie
Senior Photography Stylist: Kay E. Clarke
Test Kitchen Director: Elizabeth Tyler Luckett
Test Kitchen Assistant Director: Julie Christopher
Recipe Editor: Gayle Hays Sadler
Contributing Test Kitchen Staff: Jennifer A. Cofield; Gretchen Feldtman, R.D.; David Gallent; Ana Price Kelly and Jan A. Smith

DESIGN
Designers: Polly Tullis Browning, Diana Sanders Cates, Cherece Athy Cooper, Peggy Elliott Cunningham, Anne Pulliam Stocks, Linda Diehl Tiano and Becky Werle
Executive Assistant: Debra Smith
Technical Assistant: Karla Edgar

ART
Art Director: Mark Hawkins
Senior Production Artist and Color Technician: Mark Potter
Production Artist: Elaine Barry
Staff Photographer: Russell Ganser
Photography Stylists: Tiffany Huffman and Janna Laughlin
Publishing Systems Administrator: Becky Riddle
Publishing Systems Assistants: Myra S. Means and Chris Wertenberger

PROMOTIONS
Associate Editor: Steven M. Cooper
Designer: Dale Rowett
Graphic Artist: Deborah Kelly

BUSINESS STAFF
Publisher: Rick Barton
Vice President, Finance: Tom Siebenmorgen
Director of Corporate Planning and Development: Laticia Mull Cornett
Vice President, Retail Marketing: Bob Humphrey
Retail Marketing Director: Margaret Sweetin
Vice President, Sales: Ray Shelgosh
Vice President, National Accounts: Pam Stebbins
Vice President, Operations: Jim Dittrich
Comptroller, Operations: Rob Thieme
Retail Customer Service Manager: Wanda Price
Print Production Manager: Fred F. Pruss

Library of Congress Catalog Number 99-71586
Hardcover ISBN 1-57486-217-0
Softcover ISBN 1-57486-218-9

10 9 8 7 6 5 4 3 2 1

Gooseberry Patch

Christmas

Book 3

A LEISURE ARTS PUBLICATION

Christmas

Gooseberry Patch

For all our Gooseberry friends…
you make every day delightful!

How Did Gooseberry Patch Get Started?

You may know the story of Gooseberry Patch...the tale of two country friends who decided one day over the backyard fence to try their hands at the mail order business. Started in JoAnn's kitchen back in 1984, Vickie & JoAnn's dream of a "Country Store in Your Mailbox" has grown and grown to a 96-page catalog with over 400 products, including cookie cutters, Santas, snowmen, gift baskets, angels and our very own line of cookbooks! What an adventure for two country friends!

Through our catalogs and books, Gooseberry Patch has met country friends from all over the world. While sharing letters and phone calls, we found that our friends love to cook, decorate, garden and craft. We've created Kate, Holly & Mary Elizabeth to represent these devoted friends who live and love the country lifestyle the way we do. They're just like you & me... they're our "Country Friends®!"

Your friends at Gooseberry Patch

Holly   Mary Elizabeth   Kate   Spotty

Just For You

Contents

Homespun Christmas Memories

There's no place like home for the holidays...and there's no better time to bring out Christmas keepsakes, the family photo albums and those greeting cards that are just too pretty to discard! You can make this year's celebration extra special by enjoying favorite family traditions, and creating exciting new ones. Get set for the most memorable holiday ever!

These holiday ornaments are the perfect way to display cherished family photographs. You can easily make your own using photo transfers of snapshots. Instructions begin on page 120.

Ann & Santa 1959

Have a "Make-It-&-Take-It" craft night. Every month, meet at a different friend's house and learn to make a craft for Christmas. By the time December rolls around, you'll have enough neat new gifts and decorations to go around! Keep the craft simple enough to complete in one night, then take home and hide for the holidays.

Be prepared for the first snow day of the year: Keep a small box filled with items needed to make a snowman...hats, mittens, woolly scarves, twigs and small lumps of coal or rocks for eyes and buttons.

Pick one room in which to do all your Christmas wrapping and crafting. Don't worry about keeping it tidy. Wrap the door to look like a package with a sign that reads "Do not open until Christmas," or "Santa's Workshop," or "Do Not Enter... Authorized Elves Only!"

Tie a big red bow on the antenna of your car. This makes it easier to find in those crowded parking lots.

Here's a great project for the kids. Save the shiny metal lids from frozen juice cans. During the year, set aside their best little photos, such as those taken at school or on their birthdays. (Double prints are great!) Take out the photos and cut the images to fit inside the lids. Help the children glue some rickrack, ribbon or lace around the edge and glue a loop of pretty fabric ribbon to the back...you'll have a Christmas ornament for Grandma & Grandpa. Or buy some disk magnets in the craft section and glue them onto the backs of the lids. Then the relatives can look at their little angels all year 'round!

You'll want to choose an extra-special photo to adorn this piecework hanging pillow! Instructions are on page 120.

A bit of German folklore...if you keep herring or cabbage in the house on New Year's Eve, you'll have money all year. If you eat a piece of herring as the clock strikes midnight, you'll be lucky all year.

An old Yugoslavian custom is to bake bread on Christmas Eve for family and friends. What is so special about this bread? After it's baked, a large gold coin is inserted inside, and when it's served, it's anyone's guess who will receive that special piece. Children especially enjoy this old-fashioned tradition for the holidays!

Animals have Christmas traditions all their own. So the legend goes, for one hour on Christmas Eve, all animals can speak.

Early American folklore says that on New Year's Day the lady of the house would open first the front door and then the back door, letting the cold air flow through the house. After a moment she would say, "letting out the old and letting in the new!"

Early settlers of Massachusetts lit their Christmas candles from the stub of a candle remaining from the previous year's Christmas.

In Victorian times, it was customary to hang a glass pickle ornament somewhere on the tree. On Christmas morning, the first child to find the pickle received a special little gift. Why not try it at your house!

According to Irish folklore, if you find a bird's nest in your Christmas tree, it is a sign of life and good fortune for the coming year.

Make these quick & easy keepsake ornaments to give to family & friends at your holiday festivities. Use paint pens to draw simple designs and handletter names, dates and seasonal messages on colorful glass balls.

'Tis the season to show off your favorite treasures. If you don't already have a collection, start one...try Santas (like ours), snowmen or Christmas cottages.

A collection of Santas looks wonderful on the shelves of a pie safe...add lots of tiny votives to cast a soft glow. Fold a red & white quilt over an open pie safe door or hang stockings from a length of jute.

Display all of your holiday books in a basket by a cozy chair. Set aside a night to gather the family around and read your favorites together.

Start a collection of Christmas books to hand down over the years. Books with Christmas themes, illustrations, stories, poems, recipes...old and new...will be treasured always. You can search new and used bookstores, garage sales and tag sales. The older books are becoming scarce, but occasionally you can find delightful old Christmas stories. Bring the books out every December to enjoy and share with family.

Dress your favorite Teddy bears in mufflers and stocking caps to form a holiday "greeting committee."

a happy memory never wears out.

—LIBBIE FUDIM—

Looking for a great way to display this year's Christmas cards? Salvage old window shutters, paint them bright red and accent with homespun and buttons. Complete instructions are on page 120.

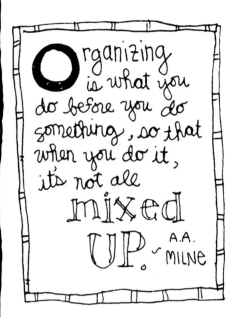

Organizing is what you do before you do something, so that when you do it, it's not all mixed UP. ~A.A. MILNE

Use pictures cut from last year's Christmas cards for this year's gift tags!

Purchase an old glass milk bottle at a flea market. Perfect for setting out once a year...for Santa's milk and cookies, of course!

A holiday keepsake: Use a permanent marker to trace your children's hands on a solid color tablecloth. Have them write their names and ages with a pencil, then embroider over the pencil lines. Gently wash to remove all pencil markings.

Help a young couple start their own Christmas collection...special ornaments, Santas and snowmen.

13

Don't forget to check the batteries in your camera! Stock up on extra batteries for toys, film, light bulbs and hooks for your ornaments.

When you have family members visiting for the holidays (especially those who live far away), get out the old picture albums, slides and family films! What a joy to reminisce together, laugh and share special memories of childhood and Christmases past!

A charming Bavarian custom: On Saint Barbara's Day (December 4), cut several branches from a flowering fruit tree, such as apple, pear or cherry, and place them in water inside the house. If the branches blossom by Christmas, legend has it, the family will be blessed in the new year.

Charming!

A favorite tradition that we have passed on to our daughter and her family involves cutting down the Christmas tree each year. We pack either a breakfast or a picnic lunch to have in the woods after we get our tree. How nice it is to have a winter picnic, complete with fire to cook bacon or hot dogs. Yum-yum!

— Carrol Begley

Craft whimsical memory album pages to complement special holiday memories, like a trip to the tree farm. Or showcase a family picture on a rustic tray with a homespun fabric mat…just the thing to give to Grandma! Instructions for both projects begin on page 120.

CHRISTMAS MAGIC

Just ask Kate, Holly & Mary Elizabeth...Christmas is the most magical time of the year! Kate likes to keep her decorations natural: popcorn and cranberries are among her favorite trims. Mary Elizabeth creates a wonderland of sweets, and Holly is crazy about Santas of all shapes and sizes. Turn the page to find lots of great holiday trims.

Ticking peppermint candy canes and felt redbirds look so nostalgic with a popcorn-and-cranberry garland. Instructions begin on page 121.

Sweet Christmas Greetings

"WELCOME HOME" DOOR PILLOW

- muslin
- fusible interfacing
- striped and plaid fabrics
- tissue paper
- gold and red embroidery floss
- fabric glue
- four buttons
- polyester fiberfill
- jute

Refer to Embroidery Stitches, page 133, before beginning project. Use 3 strands of floss for all embroidery.

1. Cut a 4¹/₂"x7" piece from muslin; pull threads to fringe edges ¹/₄-inch. Cut a 3"x6" piece from interfacing. Cut two 7"x9¹/₂" pieces from striped fabric for pillow front and back. Tear one ¹/₂"x6" strip from plaid fabric for hanger; tear two ¹/₂"x3¹/₂" and two ¹/₂"x6¹/₂" strips from plaid fabric for trim.

2. Trace Welcome Home pattern, page 142, onto tissue paper. Center and pin pattern on muslin. Using red floss, work *Back Stitches* over words. Use gold floss to work *Running Stitches, Straight Stitches* and *French Knots* over star and sprinkles; carefully tear away paper.

3. Center and fuse interfacing on wrong side of stitched piece. Overlapping ends, glue strips around stitched area.

4. Center muslin on right side of one pillow piece. Use floss to sew one button at each corner of strips to attach stitched piece to pillow front.

5. Leaving an opening for turning, matching right sides and catching ends of hanger in seam at top of pillow, use a ¹/₂-inch seam allowance to sew pillow pieces together. Turn pillow right side out. Lightly stuff pillow with fiberfill and sew opening closed.

6. Tie a length of jute into a bow…tack bow at top center of pillow.

Welcome one & all to your holiday home with the smiling faces of your family! Just trim a grapevine door basket with greenery and snapshots framed with paper-doily snowflakes. See page 121 for instructions.

Snowy day delights

Remember how much fun you had making those paper fold-and-snip snowflakes? You'll love them just as much today. Hang them in a window to celebrate the first snowfall… or choose especially pretty ones to frame. You'll find the instructions on page 122.

Kids will enjoy Christmas snow cones! Gather a pail of freshly fallen snow and top with their favorite flavor fruit juice. Make an old-fashioned treat by drizzling warm maple syrup over a bowl of fresh snow.

Dear Santa

The jolly old elf we love so much always brings warm feelings to the Christmas season. Add to the nostalgia with our collection of handmade ornaments and homespun decorations.

STENCILED SANTAS

For each shelf sitter, use the patterns on page 138, and follow *Making Patterns*, page 134, to make an entire Santa pattern and an oval pattern. Follow *Stenciling*, page 134, to make stencils, then stencil Santa on muslin. Lightly paint red cheeks, black eyes, a black line for nose, pink ears on lamb, and berries on hat; allow to dry.

Cut out Santa ³/₄-inch outside painted lines. Using painted piece as a pattern, cut out another piece from muslin for the back. Matching right sides and raw edges and leaving bottom edge open, sew pieces together using a ¹/₄-inch seam allowance; clip curves and turn right side out. Press bottom edge ¹/₄-inch to the wrong side. Stuff Santa with fiberfill to one inch from bottom. For base, draw around oval pattern on muslin, then cut out ¹/₂-inch outside drawn line; clip curves and press edge ¹/₂-inch to the wrong side.

Leaving an opening for filling, stitch base to bottom of Santa. Fill Santa with plastic filler beads and sew opening closed. Thread a bell onto 5 inches of ribbon, tie into a bow and sew to tip of hat.

For each ornament, stencil top of Santa onto muslin; cut out ³/₄-inch outside painted lines. Draw around the piece on batting, poster board and muslin; cut out pieces ³/₄-inch inside drawn lines. Center batting, then poster board on the wrong side of the painted piece; clip curves and glue the edges to the back. Glue the remaining muslin piece over the back. Making a loop at top for a hanger, hot glue jute along the edges of the ornament. Thread a bell onto 5 inches of ribbon, tie into a bow and sew to tip of hat.

Each of these jolly gentlemen has a one-of-a-kind look because you shape them by hand using paper maché.

WOODSY SANTAS

- bobby pins
- aluminum foil
- toothpick
- paintbrushes
- white gesso
- soft cloth
- assorted colors of acrylic paint
- brown water base stain
- instant paper maché
- matte clear acrylic spray
- craft glue (optional)
- glitter (optional)

Allow gesso, paint, stain and sealer to dry after each application.

1. For each ornament, slightly separate the prongs of a bobby pin.

2. Leaving top ¹/₂-inch of the pin exposed for a hanger, wrap and crush a 12-inch square of aluminum foil firmly around pin prongs. Wrap additional aluminum foil around shape as needed to form a 3 to 4-inch long head.

3. Follow manufacturer's instructions to mix paper maché. Apply an ¹/₈-inch thick layer of paper maché over aluminum foil, smoothing with finger. Use additional paper maché to sculpt nose, hat and hat trim as desired.

4. Use a toothpick to carve details into beard and hat; hang ornament to dry.

5. After ornament is thoroughly dry, apply a coat of gesso to ornament. Paint ornament as desired.

6. Apply stain to ornament and immediately wipe off excess with a soft cloth. If glitter is desired, spread a thin coat of glue over area to be covered; apply glitter to glue-covered area, then gently shake excess glitter from ornament and allow to dry. Apply 2 to 3 coats of sealer to ornament.

I collect Santas and my prize one was bought in 1938, the year I married. He followed us everywhere the Navy sent us...the first on our tree, the last off. My husband and I had 57 years together, and our Santa is still around; somewhat tarnished, but so loved.

— Mae Blevins
Oak Harbor, WA

When I was a child, I loved candy-coated milk chocolate candies, so Santa filled my whole stocking with just those! Children may have favorites that they would like delivered that way as well.

— Martha Terrell

There is no remedy for love ♡ but to love more. -THOREAU-

BUTTON ORNAMENT

- 4-inch diameter paper maché ornament with hanger
- green acrylic paint
- paintbrushes
- Santa face motif
- craft glue
- assorted red buttons
- hot glue gun
- homespun fabric strip

1. Paint ornament green and allow to dry.

2. Mix one part glue with one part water. Use glue mixture to glue Santa motif to ornament. Smooth motif in place and apply one coat of glue mixture over motif; allow to dry.

3. Layering buttons as desired and framing Santa motif, hot glue buttons to ornament.

4. Tie fabric strip into a bow around ornament hanger.

Ornaments can be stored inside a locking plastic bag. Leave a little air in the bag when you seal it, and you will provide a cushion for the ornament. Don't blow into the bag however; this creates moisture which may damage the ornament.

JOLLY BUTTON FRAME

Santa's little cherry nose is cute as a button…and so is this festive frame! Extra easy to make, it goes together in no time. Simply spray paint a wooden picture frame green and hot glue lots of red buttons over the frame…make sure you layer some buttons on top of others. This is a great quick & easy craft to do with the kids…just make sure you use a low temperature glue gun to protect little fingers.

Here's a neat way to show off your collection of antique buttons: Thread narrow satin ribbon through the button holes and tie onto the branches of a tabletop tree.

Spotty strings jute across his windows & mantel and hangs up his Christmas cards with painted clip clothespins.

SANTA TREE FENCE

A whimsical picket fence around your tree says "No peeking!" Make this jolly row of Santas with some wired picket fencing painted red, then add a band of paint to each picket for the face. The fluffy beards are torn triangles of cotton batting hot glued around the pickets...use the cotton batting to make the hat bands, too. For each mustache, knot a length of thread around the center of about eight pieces of 6-inch long yarn...glue the mustache to the fence and trim it as desired. Add painted eyes (a new eraser on a pencil works great for this) and your Santa security is ready for patrol.

WARM THOUGHTS JAR

'Twas a month before Christmas and all through the land, sweet and warm thoughts were close at hand. The Warm Thoughts Jar, such a holiday treat…to top it all off, you get something to eat!

Photocopy the warm thoughts label, page 139, onto card stock. Use a red marker to color the checkerboard border, then glue it to the front of a jar with a lid. Draw around the lid on the wrong side of a piece of homespun. Cut out the circle 1¹/₂-inches outside the drawn line. Hot glue a ball of fiberfill to the top of the lid. Cover the lid with the fabric circle and glue the edges to the sides of the lid; trim the fabric even with the lid. Place the lid on the jar and glue a length of homespun trim around the edge of the lid. Use raffia to attach a Woodsy Santa from page 24 to the jar.

Use decorative-edge craft scissors to cut out twenty-four 1"x1¹/₂" pieces of paper. Fold each piece in half and punch a ¹/₈-inch diameter hole through one corner of the folded edge. Write your warm Christmas thoughts on the papers and tie them to tissue-wrapped candies. Fill the jar with the warm thoughts.

Beginning on December 1ˢᵗ, read one wish a day to remind you of the warmth of the season and to count down to Santa's arrival.

Peppermint Dreams

It just wouldn't be Christmas without peppermints and gumdrops! Why not use these colorful candies to trim a tiny tree or glue them to foam balls to create sweet kissing balls.

How stripes get on the peppermints

GUMDROP KISSING BALL

Use a ¼-inch diameter dowel rod to push a hole all the way through a 4-inch diameter plastic foam ball. For the hanger, knot the ends of a 24-inch length of ⅝-inch wide ribbon together to form a loop; use dowel to push the loop through the hole in the ball. Hot glue the knot of the hanger to the bottom of the ball. Using hot glue, add gumdrops to the ball until it's completely covered. Tie a length of ribbon into a bow around the hanger at the top of the ball.

CANDY ORNAMENTS

The kids will love to help make these quick & easy sweet ornaments! Simply hot glue gumdrops, red hots or broken pieces of peppermint sticks over a 2-inch diameter plastic foam ball. Use ¼-inch wide grosgrain ribbon to make a hanging loop; overlap the ends and thread them onto a large head straight pin that matches the ribbon color. Use the same ribbon to make a bow with lots of loops. Thread the center of the bow onto the pin. Apply a little hot glue to the pin and stick it onto the ornament.

Re-create the joy of going to an old-fashioned candy store. Gather together several old-time canning jars and fill them with all sorts of wonderful holiday treats! Nestle among some greenery…a tempting display!

— Stacey Spaseff
Lakewood, CA

A quick & easy craft…hot glue two candy canes together; add a bow and a jingle bell and hang on the tree.

CANDY TREE

A real "kid can do" project…glue tips from gumdrops to round peppermint candies, then glue candies to ribbon bows. Attach your ornaments to a miniature tree using hot glue. Thread colorful jelly beans on string for a garland, then finish with a pinked ticking tree skirt…so sweet!

String an assortment of ribbon candy onto a holiday wreath. Your family will love to snip off a treat!

To bring up a child in the way he should go, travel that way yourself once in a while.
—JOSH BILLINGS—

For colorful fun with Christmas treats, layer different candies in a glass jar, paint the lid red and top it off with a peppermint bow.

Nothing you do for children is ever wasted.
—GARRISON KEILLOR

PEPPERMINT TOPIARY

Fill a 3-inch tall can with plaster of paris…insert a 1/2-inch diameter, 10-inch long dowel in center and allow plaster to harden. Slide a 4-inch diameter plastic foam ball 2 1/2 inches onto top of dowel. Wrap the dowel with ribbon and glue ends to secure. Glue candy sticks around the outside of the can; glue round candies on top of the can. Glue edges of round candies in rows on foam ball until ball is completely covered. Finish off your topiary with a festive red bow tied around the dowel.

By the Chimney with Care

If you're like Kate, you can't wait to see what Santa stuffs in your stocking! Hang your roomiest sock on the mantel, but also place little stocking ornaments on your tree and occasionally slip tiny surprises into them. Your family will enjoy peeking inside all season long! Instructions begin on page 122.

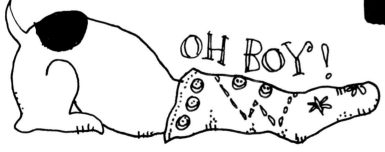

OH BOY!

"The stockings were hung by the chimney with care, in hopes that Saint Nicholas soon would be there…"

— Clement Clarke Moore

A friendly snowman and Santa fill these country stockings with holiday cheer. Knitting instructions begin on page 122.

Dreaming of a White Christmas

Seems like there's nothing better for making special memories than the excitement a Christmas snow brings. Use pearly buttons and homespun fabrics to fill your home with snowy decorations like our button candle, nostalgic ticking tree and lace-trimmed stocking. These and other simple projects are sure to turn your home into a winter wonderland the whole family will enjoy!

An assortment of pearl buttons and a cheery bow make this simple-to-create holiday wreath a wintry welcome. Instructions begin on page 124.

DREAMY WHITE CANDLE COLLECTION

Mix a few slightly weathered wooden candlesticks with lots of assorted crystal candleholders. Topped with white candles and tucked between sprigs of greenery, they're perfect for a mantel or table centerpiece! You can create your own "weathered" candlesticks using wooden spindles or pillars. Sand the wooden pieces until smooth and clean, then paint brown. Apply a thin coat of paste floor wax and a topcoat of white paint; let paint dry between coats. Lightly sand each candleholder for a beautiful aged look.

QUICK and EASY CANDLES

BUTTON CANDLE

This candle is so easy to make that Kate used dozens to decorate her house! Start with a plain pillar candle and an assortment of white buttons, then begin gluing…hot glue works best. Be creative! Use the buttons to make designs or you could even layer buttons, too.

Line the steps of an open staircase with layers of fresh cedar sprigs and scented candles in votive holders. You can also stencil on white lunch-size paper sacks, then fill the sacks partially with sand and set a votive inside each one.

"Peace, like charity, begins at home."

— Franklin Roosevelt

 Give a tabletop tree country charm using star ornaments, handmade of ticking. Why not make a matching tree topper and skirt, too? Instructions begin on page 41.

Paper-white narcissus bulbs are easy to plant and fast-growing, too! Plant about 4 to 6 weeks before Christmas and you'll have an explosion of tiny white, fragrant flowers for your holiday table.

Create a lacy border for the mantel...use white shelf paper and cut a decorative border along one edge, then add lots of fresh pine and white candles.

TICKING TREE

Tree Topper Star

- tracing paper
- tan ticking
- buttons
- embroidery floss
- polyester fiberfill
- pinking shears

1. Trace large star pattern, page 142, onto tracing paper. Use pattern to cut 2 stars from ticking.

2. Sew a cluster of buttons at center on right side of one star shape.

3. Matching wrong sides and leaving an opening for stuffing, use 3 strands of floss to work *Running Stitches*, page 133, along the edges of the star to sew pieces together.

4. Lightly stuff star with fiberfill, then sew opening closed. Use pinking shears to trim edges of star.

(Star Ornaments & Tree Skirt continued on page 124)

A vintage ornament box lets you share a collection of sweet memories, while still keeping them safe. Making arrangements of your favorite ornaments is a sentimental reminder of precious holiday memories.

Antique lace and buttons dress up a stocking made from cotton ticking. Instructions begin on page 125.

EMBOSSED CARDS

Embossing adds a charming personal touch to blank cards. Place the card wrong side up on a metal stencil. Use a stylus to rub over the design...don't be afraid to use a little pressure so you'll get a good imprint. Use the cards yourself, or give a set as a gift!

COUNTRY GIFT WRAP

Perfect for your special hand-delivered gifts! Adorn your surprises in simple ticking or sponge-painted gift wrap. Using acrylic paint and a 1½-inch square sponge piece, follow the easy *Sponge Painting* instructions, page 134, to decorate white paper. Wrap your gift in fabric or painted paper, tie it closed with raffia and hot glue a pretty button to the raffia knot. For a gift tag, write your message on card stock, glue it to a larger piece of ticking-covered card stock, then add buttons.

CROSS-STITCHED ORNAMENTS

- embroidery floss
  (see color key for desired
  design, page 145)
- 3¹/₄"x4" piece of 18-ct Aida
- green felt
- pinking shears
- flannel fabric
- buttons
- black craft wire

*Refer to Cross Stitch, page 132, and Embroidery
Stitches, page 133, before beginning project.*

1. Using 2 strands of floss for *Cross Stitches* and
one strand of floss for *Backstitches* and *French
Knots*, center and stitch desired design from
pages 144-145 on Aida.

2. Cut two 4³/₄"x5¹/₄" pieces from felt. Use pinking
shears to cut a 4"x4³/₄" piece from flannel. Center
and pin the flannel, then the stitched piece on one
felt piece. Use 6 strands of red floss to work *Blanket*

Trim a country tree with charming cross-stitched ornaments on flannel patches. Our friendly reindeer, snow woman, gingerbread boy, angel, snowman and Santa are eager to spread holiday cheer! Finished with curly wire hangers, they'll be enjoyed for years to come!

Stitches along the edges of the stitched piece to sew the pieces together. Add buttons, bells and floss bows as desired.

3. Layer the felt pieces together. Use 6 strands of red floss to work *Blanket Stitches* along edges of the felt pieces to sew the pieces together.

4. Curl the center of a 10-inch length of wire. Thread a button onto each end of the wire. Poke the ends of the wire through the top corners of the ornament, then coil the ends to secure.

Fresh Traditions

This Christmas, decorate your tables with beautiful centerpieces featuring colorful fruit and fragrant evergreens arranged in vintage bowls or pretty glass serving pieces. Include candles to provide a warm holiday glow.

FRUIT CENTERPIECE

Create a healthy centerpiece brimming with all the best of an old-fashioned Christmas...arrange seasonal fruits and greenery on a clear glass cake stand (you may need to use a piece of floral foam and floral picks to secure the fruit). Hollow out some of the fruit for clever votive holders.

NESTLED FRUIT BOWLS

Choose a large and a small yellowware bowl from Grandma's cupboard. Fill the bowls with your favorite fresh fruits, and stack the small bowl on top of the large one. Tuck greenery between the fruit to fill any empty spaces.

FRUITFUL WREATH

To welcome visitors with an inviting door wreath, hot glue fresh greenery and berries to an 18-inch diameter grapevine wreath and use floral picks to attach colorful fresh fruit. Follow the instructions on page 132 to top off the look with a cheery red bow. Our bow used nine 8-inch loops, a center loop and four 7-inch streamers. Wire the bow in place on the wreath.

TOPIARIES

FRESH FRUIT TOPIARIES

Paint 6-inch diameter clay pots as desired with acrylic paint, let dry and spray with clear sealer. Fill pots with floral foam. Insert and glue a 1/2-inch diameter, 15-inch long twig in the center of the foam. Fill the pots with greenery and fruit; use greenery pins and floral picks to secure in place, if necessary. For apple topper, glue a 4-inch diameter plastic foam ball onto top 3 inches of the twig. Use floral picks to attach apples to ball; fill between apples with greenery. For wreath topper, slide and glue the bottom of a 6-inch diameter grapevine wreath onto the top of the twig…hot glue greenery to the wreath.

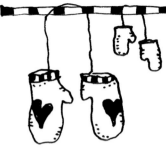

HANGING JAR LUMINARIES

Create a warm welcome for guests with glass jar luminaries. Using 2 lengths of heavy-duty wire, wrap one around each side of a jar. Twist the ends together on each side to tighten the wires under the lip of the opening…bend the ends to form hooks. Loop ends of another length of heavy-duty wire through the hooks to form a handle. Wrap black craft wire around the handle for decoration…bend the ends to form spirals, squiggles and curly-q's! Add a homespun bow, greenery and miniature pine cones at one side of the handle, then fill jar with rose hips and a votive candle.

Make it an herbal Christmas…garlands, topiaries, fragrant trees and wreaths, spicy pomanders, bundles of herbs, berries, dried apples, oranges, red roses and potpourris all bring wonderful scents to your holiday home.

LANTERN NIGHTLIGHT

Re-create the glow of an old, oil-burning lantern from yesteryear. Remove the wick hardware from a clean lantern and replace it with a candelabra-size, clip-on lamp kit with a flickering bulb. Cut a piece of candelabra base cover to fit in the space between the base of the lantern and the bottom of the lamp kit socket. Fill the base with sand to weight it down, glue sprigs of artificial greenery to the top and then tie on a homespun bow.

An antique lantern and a chicken feeder filled with candles become nostalgic holiday decorations when surrounded with fresh greenery, colorful fruit and cheery homespun bows. Instructions for the feeder begin on page 125.

51

Pinecone Firestarters

* PARAFFIN
* RED OR GREEN WAX DYE USED IN CANDLE·MAKING
* SCENTED OIL ~ CINNAMON, BAYBERRY OR CITRUS SPICE
* DRIED PINECONES
* CANDLEWICK

1. melt paraffin in coffee can placed in an electric skillet filled with water. Add colored wax dye & drops of oil to melted paraffin.

2. Wrap or tie a length of candlewick through top of the pinecone. Dip dried pinecones into melted paraffin. You may need to dip several times; allow to harden between dips.

3. Package in a basket or decorated bag ~ add a tag that reads, "PLACE SEVERAL PINECONES UNDER LOGS and LIGHT THEM."

Scented pine cone firestarters create a warm and friendly atmosphere. To make a festive gift tag, photocopy the label on page 157 and glue it to fabric-covered cardboard with fringed edges.

WREATH ORNAMENTS

Craft one of our mini wreath ornaments in a jiffy! Glue artificial leaves and berries, miniature pine cones or grapevine stars and buttons onto a 4-inch diameter grapevine wreath…add a homespun hanger and a jute bow to each ornament and they are ready to hang!

A wooden bowl filled with pomegranates, lady apples and juniper makes a welcoming country centerpiece.

Add greenery sprigs to lunch-size brown paper sacks, tuck in berries and display on your mantel.

For a magical show of colorful flames in the fireplace, soak your pine cones in the following solution before making them into firestarters: Mix $1/2$ lb. soda, borax or salt with $1/2$ gallon water. Soak cones overnight, remove from solution and hang in a mesh bag to dry thoroughly. In your fireplace, the pine cones will burn different colors.

— Joan Schaeffer

Create simple, old-fashioned holiday greetings…fill a pitcher with greenery, berries and twigs, pile pine cones in a bowl or tie decorated mini grapevine wreaths with homespun.

Hand made from the Heart

Sharing handmade gifts with special people is the best part of Christmas! Give whimsical kitchen accessories to a favorite cook, or surprise snow pals with cozy appliquéd sweatshirts. We've also included delightful packaging ideas and homemade cards, and the kids can get into the spirit with fun activities and presents they make for their friends. And don't forget the family pets!

Homespun fabrics peek through country cut-outs on these clever cards! Mail them to friends or make a set to give as a gift. Instructions for our gift tags and cards begin on page 125.

...mas comes but
...a year...

Aunt
Mary

to:
from:

...mas comes but
...ce a year...

to:
from:

from:

M a t t

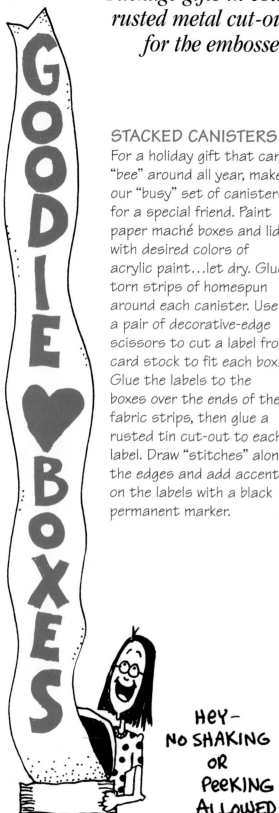

Package gifts in country style using boxes trimmed with rusted metal cut-outs or embossed copper. Instructions for the embossed-copper boxes are on page 126.

STACKED CANISTERS

For a holiday gift that can "bee" around all year, make our "busy" set of canisters for a special friend. Paint paper maché boxes and lids with desired colors of acrylic paint…let dry. Glue torn strips of homespun around each canister. Use a pair of decorative-edge scissors to cut a label from card stock to fit each box. Glue the labels to the boxes over the ends of the fabric strips, then glue a rusted tin cut-out to each label. Draw "stitches" along the edges and add accents on the labels with a black permanent marker.

HEY—
NO SHAKING
OR
PEEKING
ALLOWED

Just Give Me 1 Teensy Hint!

Nothing is more appreciated than a thoughtful gift. Think of the recipient's interests, loves and hobbies. Dream up a gift, big or small, to reflect those likes and loves. Reflect on something out-of-the-ordinary. Use your imagination.

Little boxes are PERFECT for little gifts! Fill 'em with potpourri, jewelry, candy... surprise a country friend with a personalized box for paper clips & rubber bands... hide a secret message inside!

Vintage Kitchen

Delight a country cook with handcrafted accessories. Our sweet angel can watch over the kitchen, and the decoupaged tray is perfect for serving goodies.

A wooden spoon is at the heart of this charming angel. Instructions begin on page 126.

Scope out your neighborhood antique shops for a beautiful teapot and hide bags of flavored tea inside.

Put together a family cookbook with fun photos on each page...Uncle Floyd in the kitchen or Grandpa asleep in the recliner after lunch. Include funny stories or quotes from relatives. Photocopy a family quilt or a familiar fabric (Grandma's kitchen curtains?) for the background paper.

Buy a plain canvas apron at the hobby store and personalize it with fabric paint. Tuck a spoon, spatula and jar of Chunky Chocolate Cookie Mix (page 80) in the pockets...fold neatly and tie with a ribbon. A fun gift for the cookie snacker or for a child just learning to bake! (Add a little bag of extra chocolate chunks for snackin'!)

Tuck a cornbread mix and hot pad inside a cast-iron skillet...a quick gift!

SERVING TRAY

- spray primer
- metal serving tray
- ivory spray paint
- ivory, red and brown acrylic paint
- paintbrushes
- crackle medium
- black paint pen
- desired Santa motifs from cards or wrapping paper
- decoupage glue
- wood-tone spray
- clear acrylic matte spray sealer

Allow primer, paint, glue and sealer to dry after each application.

1. Apply primer to tray. Spray paint sides and rim of tray ivory. Using brown for basecoat and ivory acrylic paint for topcoat, follow manufacturer's instructions to crackle the bottom of the tray.

2. Use the paint pen to draw the outer edges of the checkerboard border around the rim of the tray. Paint every other square red, then go over the edges of the squares with the paint pen. Write your favorite words of the season along the sides of the tray.

3. Trim motifs as desired, then glue in place on tray. Apply 2 coats of glue over motifs.

4. Lightly spray tray with wood-tone spray. Apply 2 coats of sealer to the tray.

GIFTS for the Kitchen

Plaid chickens bring pocketfuls of fun to a whimsical apron set with matching oven mitt. Easy-to-fuse appliqués also perk up our trio of kitchen towels.

OVEN MITT AND APRON

Don't be chicken to try your hand at these easy kitchen accessories! Start with a purchased apron and oven mitt and add appliqués and buttons.

For the oven mitt, cut a strip of homespun to fit along the cuff of the mitt; press the edges of the strip ¼-inch to the wrong side. Use nylon thread to sew the strip to the mitt...add a few buttons and this "handy" gift is done in no time.

For the apron, follow the mitt instructions to attach a strip of fabric across the bib. Cut two 1½"x10" and two 8½"x10" pieces from fabrics. Using a ½-inch seam allowance, sew the pieces together to form two 9"x10" pockets...press each edge ¼-inch to the wrong side. Top stitch along the top edge of each pocket. Using the patterns, page 150, follow *Making Appliqués*, page 134, to make two (one in reverse) complete chicken appliqués from fabrics. Fuse one set of appliqués to each pocket...follow *Machine Appliqué*, page 134, to sew along the edges of the appliqués.

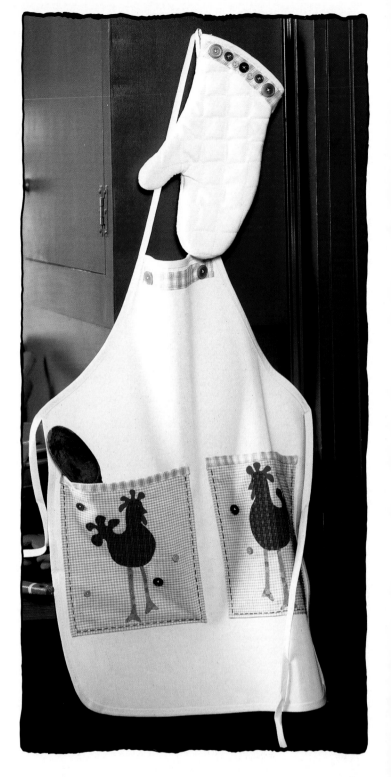

Pin the pockets on the apron and *Machine Appliqué* the sides and bottom edges. Referring to *Embroidery Stitches*, page 133, use green floss to work *Running Stitches* along the side and bottom edges of the pockets and gold floss to work *French Knots* for the eyes on the chickens. Sew buttons on the pockets and bib as desired.

APPLIQUÉ TEA TOWELS

For each towel, use a ½" seam allowance to sew three 4"x5" pieces of fabric together to form a 5"x10" rectangle. Using the patterns on pages 150-151, follow *Making Appliqués*, page 134, to make desired appliqués from fabrics. Fuse appliqués on rectangle, then follow *Machine Appliqué*, page 134, to sew along the edges of the appliqués. Fuse a 5"x10" piece of paper-backed fusible web to the back of the rectangle. Center and fuse the rectangle on one end of an 18"x28" kitchen towel. *Machine Appliqué* along the edges of the rectangle. Referring to *Embroidery Stitches*, page 133, use 3 strands of green floss to work *Running Stitches* along the edges of the rectangle and gold floss to work *French Knots* and *Straight Stitches* as indicated on the patterns. Sew a button to each corner of the rectangle.

"Live your life while you have it. Life is a splendid gift — there is nothing small about it."
— Florence Nightengale

Winter Warmers

Even when the weather outside is frightful, these merry shirts are so delightful! Raid the button box to find colorful "ornaments" for the embroidered tree and whimsical "snowflakes" for the sweatshirts, or string buttons for a fun-to-wear necklace. Instructions for the clothing begin on page 126.

BUTTON NECKLACE

Fold a 6-foot length of waxed linen thread in half. Knot the folded end to form a small loop. Measure 4 inches from the knot and knot again. Hook the loop on something, like your friend's finger (we hooked ours in the ring of a binder). Place a needle on each end of the thread. Working from opposite sides, thread the needles through the same hole on a button (Fig. 1). Now, thread the needles through the opposite hole of the same button (Fig. 2). Pull the threads to slide the button to the knot. Repeat to add as many buttons as you like, then knot the threads together close to the last button. For the clasp, choose a button that will fit through your loop. Insert the thread ends up, then back down through opposite hole in the button; knot the ends around the thread to secure.

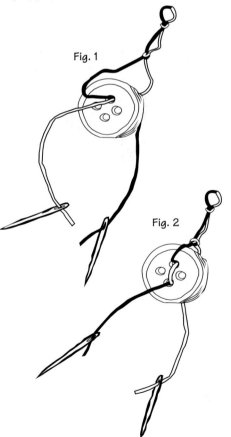

Fig. 1

Fig. 2

Cozy Comforts

When the cold wind blows, warm a friend's heart with these homespun pillows. Accent the friendly country cushions with buttons, appliqués and simple embroidery stitches.

Tuck holiday wishes in the pillow pocket for Santa's elves to find. Instructions for the Star Pillow are on page 127.

THROW PILLOWS

- fabric for pillow fronts, backs and welting
- paper-backed fusible web
- embroidery floss
- burlap scraps
- polyester fiberfill
- red buttons
- 1/4-inch dia. cord
- red, green & brown felt

Use a 1/2-inch seam allowance for all sewing.

Tree Pillow

1. For pillow top, cut four 7"x9" pieces from fabrics.

2. For each strip, matching right sides and short edges, sew two pieces together; repeat for remaining pieces. Matching right sides and long edges, sew strips together. Cut a piece from fabric the same size as pillow top for pillow back.

(continued on page 127)

Here's a neat gift for a college student: Buy a big canvas stocking and paint it in school colors...fill with ornaments, garlands and lights for the dorm room. Include a Christmas CD and a batch of homemade cookies, too!

Sort through your family's closets and donate "gently worn" and outgrown coats, clothes and extra blankets to a nearby shelter. They'll be much appreciated!

Lots of FUN for the Little Ones

Let the kids get in on the fun of Christmas crafting…including handmade gifts for their friends. With a little help from you, youngsters can put together a "make-it-yourself" Christmas card kit or a colorful play dough set to inspire the imagination. Instructions begin on page 128.

Magic Reindeer Dust

KIDS' NUTTY Snowmen

...Make a whole bowl-full to hang on the tree!

You will need:

* Unsalted peanuts-in-the-shell
* Acrylic paint - white
* Small paint brush
* Fine-tip black permanent marker
* Fine-tip red permanent marker
* Red yarn
* Safety scissors

1. Pour peanuts out on a newspaper and let the kids paint 'em white. Let peanuts dry and eat a hand-full while you wait!

2. Use your markers to draw on eyes, nose & mouth — add buttons on the front of the snow peanuts, too!

3. Cut a 5" piece of yarn and tie it 'round your snowman's neck. All done!

*P.S. Thread a thin ribbon or fishing line through the back of the yarn to make a hanger.

Secret Ingredients!
* OATS (FOR ANIMALS)
* GLITTER
* PINT-SIZE CANNING JAR WITH LID

Secret How-To Instructions:

1. Fill jars with oats, sprinkling a little glitter throughout.

2. Top jars with lids and tie on a copy of "Secret Instructions for Magic Reindeer Dust" (below). You might glue it on jar, if preferred.

*Make a Copy of this for each jar ↓

Magic Reindeer Dust

Come December 24th, as Santa flies here from the North,
Here's what you do, it isn't hard —
Just sprinkle this stuff in your yard...

The sparkles draw old Santa near
and oats attract his 8 reindeer...

Then just you wait — they're on their way

P.S. Happy Holidays!

EASY RECIPES

Mary Elizabeth's Super-Duper Play Dough

Great-smelling dough ~ perfect birthday party favors!

- 2-½ c. flour
- ½ c. salt
- 1 T. powdered alum
- 2 pkg. unsweetened fruit-flavored drink mix
- 2 T. vegetable oil
- 2 c. boiling water

Mix together flour, salt, alum & drink mix in large mixing bowl. Add oil. Pour boiling water over flour mixture ~ stir until well-combined. Knead dough until smooth. Store in airtight plastic bag or covered container.

all our favorite ingredients are in my Nutty Cocoa

~ peanut butter, chocolate and marshmallows!

- 4 c. MILK
- ½ c. CHOCOLATE-FLAVORED DRINK MIX
- ¼ c. CREAMY PEANUT BUTTER
- ½ t. VANILLA
- MINIATURE MARSHMALLOWS

In a saucepan, combine chocolate mix with 1-½ c. milk until well-blended. Mix in peanut butter, and add remaining milk. Heat cocoa 'til almost boiling. Pour into mugs and top with marshmallows.

Old-fashioned CANDLE SALAD

~ a fun fruit salad for kids to make for a holiday dinner!

- BIBB LETTUCE LEAVES
- CANNED PINEAPPLE RINGS
- BANANAS
- WHIPPED TOPPING
- MARASCHINO CHERRIES

Place one lettuce leaf on each plate. Lay a pineapple slice on top of lettuce. Cut banana in half and stand in hole of each pineapple ring. Top each banana with a dab of whipped topping ~ put cherry on top of whipped topping. Beautiful!

Make fun containers for your play dough using baby food jars and our label design on page 143. Color the photocopied artwork with permanent markers and acrylic paint.

SANTA SHAKES

MAKE UP A BATCH OF THIS COOL YOGURT SHAKE TO REFRESH THE KIDS AFTER THEY FINISH MAKING NUTTY SNOWMEN!

- 2 CUPS CHOCOLATE MILK
- 2 CUPS CHOCOLATE FROZEN YOGURT, SOFTENED
- 2 CUPS CRUSHED ICE
- ½ CUP CHOCOLATE SYRUP
- PEPPERMINTS, CRUSHED
- PEPPERMINT STICKS OR CANDY CANES

Combine all ingredients in a blender. Process until well-blended. Sprinkle with crushed peppermint and serve in tall glasses with a candy cane.

Kate's Best-ever Chocolate Finger Paint

FOR THE BUDDING ARTIST IN ALL OF US ~ THE TASTIEST FINGER PAINT OF ALL! TRY VANILLA OR BUTTERSCOTCH, TOO....

4-oz. PKG. instant chocolate pudding mix

2 c. milk
white paper

Prepare pudding mix according to package directions. Let the pudding set 'til thick. Paint on white paper with pudding. Let masterpieces dry for several hours.

RAINBOW Toast

IS IT MORE FUN TO MAKE IT OR EAT IT?

- BREAD
- FOOD COLORING
- CLEAN PAINTBRUSHES OR COTTON SWABS

PLACE 4 DROPS OF FOOD COLORING IN EACH SECTION OF A MUFFIN TIN. ADD 1 TO 2 T. WATER TO DILUTE COLORS. DIP PAINTBRUSH INTO FOOD COLORING AND PAINT DESIGNS ON BREAD. PLACE IN TOASTER AND TOAST. BUTTER & EAT IT UP!

KATE'S TORTILLA TREATS

A PERFECT SNACK FOR YOUR HUNGRY YOUNG BUILDERS!

INGREDIENTS:

- FLOUR TORTILLAS
- PEANUT BUTTER
- MINI CHOCOLATE CHIPS

HOW TO:

SIMPLY SPREAD THE PEANUT BUTTER ON THE OPEN TORTILLA.

SPRINKLE CHOCOLATE CHIPS ON THE PEANUT BUTTER, THEN ROLL UP THE TORTILLA.

SCRUMPTIOUS!

PIZZA COBBLER

KIDS LOVE TO FIX

~ an easy and delicious snack!

- PIZZA SAUCE
- 1 CAN REFRIGERATOR BISCUITS
- 1-⅓ c. MOZZARELLA CHEESE, SHREDDED

GREASE AN 8-INCH SQUARE PAN WITH VEGETABLE OIL SPRAY. PLACE ABOUT ¼ OF THE PIZZA SAUCE IN BOTTOM OF THE PAN. CUT EACH BISCUIT IN 4 PIECES. ROLL BISCUIT PIECES INTO BALLS AND PLACE IN PAN ON TOP OF SAUCE. POUR REMAINING SAUCE OVER BISCUITS. SPRINKLE WITH MOZZARELLA CHEESE. BAKE IN 400° OVEN FOR 15 TO 20 MINUTES. ENJOY!

Pampered Pets

Pets are family too! Include them in your holiday celebration with tasty treats and other fun gifts.

HEALTHY DOG TREATS

Visiting in a dog lover's home? Bring along some homemade, easy to bake dog biscuits.

2 c. whole-wheat flour
1/2 c. all-purpose flour
1/4 c. cornmeal
1/4 c. sunflower kernels, finely
    chopped
1 t. salt
1/4 c. molasses
2 eggs, beaten
1/4 c. milk
2 T. oil

Mix all ingredients, adding more milk if needed to make dough firm. Roll out onto a floured surface to a 1/2-inch thickness. Use any shape cookie cutter to cut out biscuits, but bone shapes are fun! Bake on ungreased baking sheets at 350 degrees for 30 minutes or until lightly toasted. To make biscuits harder, leave in oven with the heat turned off for an hour or more.

Jacqueline Lash-Idler
Rockaway, NJ

For a doggone cute tree ornament, use paint pens and ribbon to decorate a dog bone…then hang it out of your pet's reach.

Any dog will love this soft, cozy bed on a cold winter's night! Instructions are on page 128.

KITTY KOOKIES

Remember that your four-legged friends love treats too.

1 c. whole-wheat flour
6-oz. can tuna in oil, undrained
1 T. oil
1 egg

Mix all ingredients in a mixing bowl, adding a little water if dough is too stiff. On a lightly floured surface, roll dough to ¹/₄-inch thickness. Cut into shapes with your favorite cookie cutter. Place on ungreased baking sheet. Bake at 350 degrees for 20 minutes or until firm. Store in an airtight container.

Give an animal the best gift of all...go to the local animal shelter and adopt a pet!

Surprise Fluffy with catnip-filled toys; instructions begin on page 129.

Use paint pens to create a festive ceramic dish for your favorite feline.

BRAIDED BIRD WREATH

Make a picnic for the birds...they'll flock to this treat, and you'll enjoy watching them.

1 lb. frozen bread dough, thawed
peanut butter
wild birdseed

Roll out dough into a 30-inch rope. Using a sharp knife, cut the dough into thirds lengthwise and braid. Place braided dough on a greased baking sheet, forming a circle. Seal the edges of dough by pinching them together. Cover with a clean dish towel and let rise one hour or until double in size. Bake at 375 degrees for 20 to 30 minutes or until golden brown. Remove from baking sheet and let cool. Spread peanut butter on top of wreath and sprinkle with birdseed. Hang outside for the birds to enjoy!

73

Goodies
for
GIVING

H and-packaged, homemade
goodies show friends & family
just how special they are to you.
Take time to remember how each
person has brightened your life as
you share a loaf of bread, a batch
of creamy fudge, or some moist,
chewy cookies made just for them!
Or open up your pantry and gather
the ingredients to make one of the
Country Friends® winning recipe
mixes for friends to enjoy after
the holidays are over. Whatever you
choose to make, dress it up in a
pretty gift basket or bag...and they
will know it was made with love!

*Nothing says, "You're special to me" like yummy homemade
Christmas treats in a country bag or basket. Recipes begin on
page 76; bag and basket instructions begin on page 130.*

ONE CUP OF EVERYTHING COOKIES

Add any of your favorite cookie ingredients!

1 c. butter, softened
1 c. sugar
1 c. brown sugar, packed
1 egg
3 c. all-purpose flour
1 c. quick-cooking oatmeal, uncooked
1 c. crispy rice cereal
1 c. semi-sweet chocolate chips
1 t. baking soda
1 t. cream of tartar
1 t. vanilla extract

Cream butter, sugars and egg together. Add remaining ingredients and stir until dough is formed. Press into one-inch balls and place on an ungreased baking sheet. Flatten balls with bottom of a greased glass. Bake at 350 degrees for 10 minutes or until bottoms are lightly browned. Makes about 6½ dozen cookies.

Claddagh Inn
Hendersonville, NC

STIR YOUR HOT TEA WITH A PEPPERMINT STICK FOR A CHRISTMAS-TIME TREAT.

CREAMY FUDGE

A delicious, creamy fudge.

12-oz. pkg. semi-sweet chocolate chips
13-oz. jar marshmallow creme
2 t. vanilla extract
2 c. chopped walnuts
5 c. sugar
1 c. butter
12-oz. can evaporated milk

Place chocolate chips, marshmallow creme, vanilla and walnuts in a mixing bowl. Heat sugar, butter and milk in a large saucepan. Bring mixture to a boil and boil for 15 minutes, stirring often. Continue to boil until mixture reaches 234 degrees or soft-ball stage on a candy thermometer. Place mixture into mixing bowl containing chips and beat on high speed until creamy. Pour into buttered 8"x8" pan. Will set in about 3 to 4 hours.

Gail Wightman

NO-COOK MINTS

Pretty holiday mints!

4³/₄ c. powdered sugar, sifted
1/3 c. corn syrup
1/4 c. butter, softened
1 t. peppermint extract
1/2 t. salt
red and green liquid food coloring

Combine powdered sugar, corn syrup, butter, peppermint extract and salt; mix with spoon and hands until smooth. Divide into thirds; knead one drop of red food coloring into one third and one drop of green food coloring into another third. Leave remaining third white. Shape into small balls; flatten with fork on wax paper-lined baking sheets. Let dry several hours. Yields 72 patties.

Joan Schaeffer
Whitefish Bay, WI

CINNAMON CRUNCH BARS

Keep on hand for the grandchildren.

12 cinnamon graham crackers, 2¹/₂"x4³/₄" each
2 c. chopped walnuts or pecans
1 c. butter
1 c. brown sugar, packed
¹/₂ t. cinnamon

In the bottom of a greased 15"x10" jelly roll pan, arrange graham crackers in a single layer with sides touching. Sprinkle nuts evenly over crackers. In a small heavy saucepan, combine butter, brown sugar and cinnamon. Stirring constantly, cook over medium heat until sugar dissolves and mixture begins to boil. Continue to boil syrup for 3 minutes longer without stirring; pour over crackers. Bake at 400 degrees for 8 to 10 minutes or until bubbly and slightly darker around the edges. Cool completely in pan; break into pieces. Store in an airtight container. Yields about 1¹/₂ pounds of candy.

Gen Hellums
Freer, TX

HONEY-GLAZED SNACK MIX

Make several batches and give in colorful tins.

4 c. oat square cereal
1¹/₂ c. pretzel twists
1 c. chopped pecans
¹/₃ c. margarine
¹/₄ c. honey

In a bowl, combine cereal, pretzels and pecans. Over low heat, melt margarine with honey until margarine is melted. Pour over mix; toss to coat. Spread on baking sheet. Bake at 350 degrees for 15 minutes. Cool and spread on wax paper.

Kathy Bolyea
Naples, FL

Slip warm holiday wishes and a loaf of hearty Cranberry Bread into a festive fabric bag. Instructions for the sawtooth-edge bag are on page 130.

CRANBERRY BREAD

Serve fresh cranberry bread with your turkey dinner.

2 c. all-purpose flour
1 c. sugar
1 1/2 t. baking powder
1/2 t. baking soda
1 t. salt
juice and zest of one orange
2 T. shortening
boiling water
1 egg, beaten
1 c. chopped walnuts
1 c. fresh cranberries, chopped

Sift dry ingredients together. In a separate bowl, combine juice, zest and shortening with enough boiling water to yield a total of 3/4 cup. Cool slightly and add egg. Blend liquid ingredients in with the dry ingredients, stirring only until flour mixture is dampened. Blend in walnuts and cranberries. Pour into one 9"x5" loaf pan coated with non-stick vegetable spray. Bake at 350 degrees for 50 minutes to one hour or until center tests done.

Judy Borecky
Escondido, CA

HOLLY'S WHITE CHOCOLATE THRILLS

These set our little ♥s to pitter-pattering!

✢

1 1/4 lb. almond bark
1 1/2 c. miniature marshmallows
1 1/2 c. peanut butter cereal
1 1/2 c. crisp rice cereal
1 1/2 c. mixed nuts
1/2 c. mini chocolate chips

. . .

In a casserole dish, melt almond bark in 200° oven for 25 minutes; stir occasionally. Place marshmallows, cereal, nuts & chocolate chips in bowl. Pour melted bark over mixture, stirring to coat. Drop by spoonfuls onto waxed paper ~ allow to set.

Take the rush out of Christmas morning for a busy family by delivering a Sour Cream Breakfast Coffee Cake ahead of time. Instructions for decorating the box are on page 131.

SOUR CREAM BREAKFAST COFFEE CAKE

My mom was busy, but she always had time for family, friends and neighbors. This is one of her best recipes.

1 c. sugar
1 c. shortening
3 eggs, beaten
1 t. vanilla extract
2¼ c. all-purpose flour
1 t. baking soda
3 t. baking powder
1 c. sour cream
²/3 c. brown sugar, packed
½ c. chopped nuts
1½ t. cinnamon

Cream sugar and shortening together. Add eggs and vanilla. Mix in flour, baking soda, baking powder and sour cream. Spread batter into a greased and floured tube pan. Mix together brown sugar, nuts and cinnamon. Spread on top of batter in pan. Bake at 375 degrees for 40 to 45 minutes or until a toothpick inserted in center comes out clean.

Mary Dungan
Gardenville, PA

A wrapped loaf of homemade bread tied to a wooden cutting board makes a heartwarming gift!

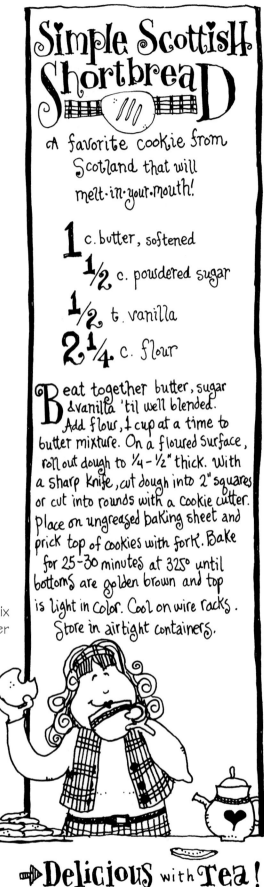

Simple Scottish Shortbread

A favorite cookie from Scotland that will melt-in-your-mouth!

1 c. butter, softened
1½ c. powdered sugar
½ t. vanilla
2¼ c. flour

Beat together butter, sugar & vanilla 'til well blended. Add flour, 1 cup at a time to butter mixture. On a floured surface, roll out dough to ¼ - ½" thick. With a sharp knife, cut dough into 2" squares or cut into rounds with a cookie cutter. Place on ungreased baking sheet and prick top of cookies with fork. Bake for 25-30 minutes at 325° until bottoms are golden brown and top is light in color. Cool on wire racks. Store in airtight containers.

➡ Delicious with Tea!

78

CRANBERRY-ORANGE CHUTNEY

An excellent relish for ham sandwiches!

4 seedless oranges
1/2 c. orange juice
1 lb. cranberries
2 c. sugar
1/4 c. crystallized ginger, diced
1/2 t. hot pepper sauce
1 cinnamon stick
1 clove garlic, peeled
3/4 t. curry powder
3/4 c. golden raisins

Peel the oranges and reserve the zest from two of them. Slice the reserved zest very thinly. Cut oranges into 1/4-inch thick slices and quarter. Combine orange zest with all remaining ingredients and simmer in a saucepan over medium heat, stirring until sugar dissolves and cranberries pop. Remove from heat and discard cinnamon and garlic clove. Add oranges and toss lightly. Serve hot or cold with ham. Makes 6 cups.

Make charming labels for canned jellies and jams using decorative-edge craft scissors, pretty papers, and markers. Dress up jar lids with colorful paper inserts.

RED PEPPER JAM

A nice hostess gift at Christmas time. I make it during the summer months and have it on hand for holiday gift-giving.

12 red peppers, seeded
2 to 4 onions, sliced
1 T. salt
2 c. vinegar
3 c. sugar

Place peppers and onions through food grinder into a saucepan. Sprinkle with salt and let stand 3 hours. Drain very well. Add vinegar and sugar and cook slowly, approximately 1 1/2 to 2 hours or until thickened. Pour mixture into clean, hot half-pint jars and process for 10 to 15 minutes in boiling water canner. Makes six half-pint jars.

Janet Myers

SUSAN'S PUMPKIN BUTTER

This recipe is very much like apple butter and has a better flavor if made with fresh pumpkin. Serve with warm, fresh bread or biscuits.

3 1/2 c. cooked or canned pumpkin
1 T. pumpkin pie spice
1 3/4-oz. box powdered fruit pectin
4 1/2 c. sugar

Place pumpkin in a large saucepan. Add pumpkin pie spice and fruit pectin to pumpkin and mix well. Place over high heat; stir until mixture comes to a gentle boil. Immediately add the sugar and stir in well. Bring to a rolling boil and boil hard for one minute, stirring constantly. Remove from heat and ladle into jars with lids. Store in refrigerator 2 to 3 weeks. Makes about 5 1/2 cups.

Elenna Firme
Haxtun, CO

THE ULTIMATE FUDGE★SAUCE

2 oz. unsweetened chocolate
3/4 c. sugar
1/4 t. salt
1/2 c. light corn syrup
1/2 c. milk
2 T. butter
1 T. vanilla

★

Combine first 5 ingredients over low heat ~ stir often. Add butter. Cool slightly, then add vanilla. oh boy!

It's A Mix, It's A Gift!

Packaged with homespun style, recipe mixes make sweet and simple gifts that offer an extra helping of holiday fun.

Delight your favorite chocoholic with our Chunky Chocolate Cookie Mix! Photocopy the artwork below and glue to a jar label and recipe tag created from decorative card stock. Instructions are on page 131.

CHUNKY CHOCOLATE COOKIE MIX

a recipe from
Melanie Lowe ★ Dover, DE

1 ¼ c. all-purpose flour
1/2 t. baking soda
½ t. salt
½ c. brown sugar, packed
⅓ c. sugar
1 ⅓ c. semi-sweet chocolate chunks
1 c. chopped pecans

Blend together flour, baking soda & salt. Spoon into bottom of a wide-mouth, one-quart canning jar, pressing down well. Layer on the remaining ingredients in the order given, packing down tightly between each layer.

CHUNKY CHOCOLATE COOKIE MIX

2/3 c. butter, softened   1 t. water
1 egg   ½ t. vanilla extract

Cream together butter, egg, water & vanilla. Add cookie mix from jar and blend well. Drop by spoonfuls on ungreased cookie sheet and bake at 375 degrees for 7 to 10 minutes. Makes about 3 dozen cookies.

How to Eat Chocolate Chip Cookies Like A Child:

HALF-SIT, HALF-LIE on the bed, propped up by a PILLOW. Read a book. Place cookies next to you on the SHEET so that CRUMBS get in the BED. As you eat the COOKIES, remove each chocolate CHIP and place it on your STOMACH. When all the cookies are consumed, eat the CHIPS one by one, allowing two per PAGE.

— DELIA ephron

♥ Choose a favorite book, slip a bookmark inside the pages and drop inside a gift bag. Now slide a jar of Cookie Mix in there and tie a copy of ← this tag on the bag handle. SILLY BUT FUN and FLAVORFUL!

WINTERTIME SPICE TEA

This is quite a favorite at our home. It's always a nice gift for teachers, friends and neighbors.

1 3/4 c. sugar
1 c. sweetened lemonade mix
1 c. powdered orange drink mix
1/2 c. instant tea
1/2 t. cinnamon
1/2 t. ground cloves

Mix all ingredients together and store in airtight container. Give recipe for serving. To serve, add 3 to 4 teaspoons to one cup of hot water; stir well.

Mary Beth Smith
St. Charles, MO

PANCAKES FROM THE PANTRY

These pancakes smell so good while they're cooking. Give with a jar of honey butter to make a really welcome gift!

4 c. quick-cooking oats, uncooked
2 c. all-purpose flour
2 c. whole-wheat flour
1 c. brown sugar, packed
1 c. dry milk
3 T. baking powder
2 T. cinnamon
5 t. salt
1/2 t. cream of tartar

Combine all ingredients together, mixing well. Add dry mix to an airtight container or to two one-quart canning jar. Add these instructions to your gift card: In a large mixing bowl, add 2 eggs; beat well. Gradually beat in 1/3 cup oil. Alternately add 2 cups of pancake mix and 1 cup of water to the egg mixture; blend well. Cook pancakes on a lightly greased griddle. Makes about 10 pancakes.

Margaret Scoresby
Mount Vernon, OH

WINTERTIME SPICE TEA
Add 3 to 4 teaspoons to one cup of hot water; stir well.

Warm up an early bird's breakfast with gifts of tea and pancake mix. For a "short stack" with style, center a ribbon under the rim of the pancake mix lid and tie the jar of maple syrup on top. Instructions for the pancake label and the Wintertime Spice Tea Cup begin on page 131.

Simple and Speedy

BASIC Bread Mix

You can use this basic mix to make 2 different breads!

a recipe from
Regina Vining
★
Warwick, RI

12 c. all-purpose flour
2 T. baking powder
2 T. baking soda
1 T. salt
3 c. sugar
3 c. brown sugar, packed

★

Sift together flour, baking powder, baking soda & salt. Stir in sugar & brown sugar until well blended. Store in a large airtight container. Place container in a cool, dry place and use within 6 months.

Feel free to copy these recipe cards and use colored pens to give them some ZING!

Orange~Berry Bread

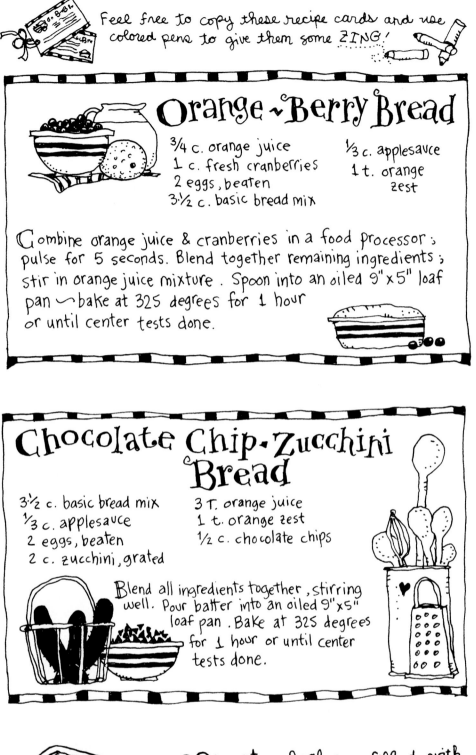

3/4 c. orange juice
1 c. fresh cranberries
2 eggs, beaten
3½ c. basic bread mix
⅓ c. applesauce
1 t. orange zest

Combine orange juice & cranberries in a food processor; pulse for 5 seconds. Blend together remaining ingredients; stir in orange juice mixture. Spoon into an oiled 9"x5" loaf pan — bake at 325 degrees for 1 hour or until center tests done.

Chocolate Chip·Zucchini Bread

3½ c. basic bread mix
⅓ c. applesauce
2 eggs, beaten
2 c. zucchini, grated
3 T. orange juice
1 t. orange zest
½ c. chocolate chips

Blend all ingredients together, stirring well. Pour batter into an oiled 9"x5" loaf pan. Bake at 325 degrees for 1 hour or until center tests done.

Present a loaf pan filled with everything the cook needs to make the two yummy breads: a can of applesauce, eggs, bags of cranberries & chocolate chips and an orange! Tie a ribbon 'round it & add the recipe cards.

HAZELNUT MOCHA MIX
Makes a great stocking stuffer!

1/4 c. plus 2 T. powdered non-dairy
    creamer
1/4 c. sugar
1/4 c. hazelnut-flavored instant
    coffee
2 T. baking cocoa

Combine all ingredients and mix
thoroughly. Spoon into a plastic
zipping bag and place in a fabric
bag for gift giving. Add these
serving instructions to your gift
tag: Place 2 tablespoons plus
2 teaspoons of mix in a mug; add
3/4 cup hot water.

Mary Lou Traylor
Arlington, TN

CHOCOLATE CHIP PIE MIX
A sweet, chocolatey treat!

1 c. sugar
1/2 c. all-purpose flour
6-oz. pkg. semi-sweet chocolate
    chips
1/2 c. flaked coconut
1/2 c. chopped pecans

Blend together sugar and flour;
place in a plastic zipping bag. Seal
bag and tie closed with a festive
ribbon and tag that says " dry
ingredients." Combine chocolate
chips, coconut and pecans in a
second plastic zipping bag and
label "chocolate packet." Tuck
both in a holiday gift bag. Add
the following instructions: In a
bowl, combine 1/4 cup melted
butter, 2 eggs and the contents
of the "dry ingredients" bag; stir
until just moistened. Stir in the
contents of the "chocolate
packet" bag. Spoon mixture into
a 9" unbaked pie crust. Bake
at 350 degrees for 35 to
40 minutes.

Kathy Grashoff
Ft. Wayne, IN

*Relatives will enjoy opening country bags holding mixtures of Chocolate Chip Pie
and Hazelnut Mocha. Fabric bag instructions begin on page 131.*

HOT ORANGE CIDER MIX
*Add an orange or apple slice to each mug
before serving.*

1 c. sugar
2 6-inch cinnamon sticks
1 whole nutmeg

Combine sugar, cinnamon sticks
and nutmeg. Place in plastic-lined
goodie bag. Add these instructions:

*Give your coffee or cider mix in a
pretty jar tucked in a tall, narrow
paper bag tied with red raffia.*

Place 2 cups apple cider and
6 cups orange juice in a slow
cooker; stir in cider mix. Turn slow
cooker to high for 2 to 3 hours or
until cider is heated through.
Remove spices before serving.

Coralita Truax
Loudonville, OH

JOLLY GINGERBREAD MEN MIX

Place a jar of this mix in a basket with a gingerbread man cookie cutter...a wonderful gift for a secret pal!

3¹/2 c. all-purpose flour, divided
1 t. baking powder
1 t. baking soda
1 c. brown sugar, packed
2 t. ginger
1 t. cinnamon
1 t. allspice

Sift together 2 cups flour, baking powder and baking soda. Spoon into a one-quart canning jar, packing down tightly. Layer on brown sugar, pushing down well. Blend together remaining flour, ginger, cinnamon and allspice; layer over brown sugar and secure lid. Tie on the following instructions: Cream together ¹/2 cup butter, ³/4 cup molasses and one egg; stir in dry mix. Dough will be stiff. Cover and refrigerate one hour. Roll dough to ¹/4-inch thickness on a lightly floured surface, adding additional flour if dough is too sticky. Cut with a 4¹/4"x3¹/2" gingerbread boy cookie cutter and place on a lightly greased baking sheet. Bake at 350 degrees for 10 to 12 minutes. Makes about 22 cookies.

Kay Morrone
Des Moines, IA

Christmas Cappuccino Mix

a recipe from Kimberly Anderson ★ Lake City, IA

2·¹/2 c. instant chocolate drink mix
8 c. dry milk
2 c. powdered sugar
1 c. instant coffee granules
8-oz. jar French vanilla flavored non-dairy creamer

★

Combine all ingredients in a large bowl, then store in an airtight container.

Cappuccino:

¹/4 to ¹/3 c. cappuccino mix
6 to 8 oz. hot water

Combine mix and hot water; stir to blend.

Help someone catch the Christmas spirit with Jolly Gingerbread Men Mix. See page 131 to make the baking instruction card.

GRANDMA'S NOODLE SOUP MIX

Add a few ingredients to this mix and you have a soup that you can enjoy in no time at all.

4 to 5 oz. fine egg noodles
3 T. chicken bouillon
salt and pepper to taste
½ t. dried thyme
½ t. celery seed
3 bay leaves

In a large mixing bowl, carefully blend together all ingredients. Add to a one-quart wide-mount canning jar; add lid. Tie on the following cooking instructions: Combine noodle soup mix and 6 cups water in a large stockpot. Add 3 carrots, diced, 2 celery stalks, chopped, and one onion, chopped. Bring to a boil, reduce heat and simmer, covered, for 20 minutes. Stir in 3 cups chicken and simmer 5 minutes longer. Remove bay leaves. Makes approximately 2 quarts soup.
Connie Hilty
Pearland, TX

Tuck your jar of noodle soup in a basket with a farmhouse bowl, a loaf of freshly-baked bread and sweet, creamy butter.

Soup and hot spicy tea make a winter meal complete!

Pizza Basket

Line a basket (or deep-dish pizza pan) with a red-checked napkin. Add:

BUSY MOM SEAL OF APPROVAL

* JARS OF PIZZA SAUCE
* DRY DOUGH MIX (BELOW)
* PACKAGES OF PEPPERONI & SHREDDED CHEESES
* FRESH VEGGIES ~ PEPPERS, ONIONS, MUSHROOMS
* PIZZA CUTTER
* RECIPE CARD FOR FAVE PIZZA

DOUGH MIX
★

11·¼ c. FLOUR, DIVIDED
3 PKGS. DRY YEAST
3 t. SUGAR
1·½ t. SALT
...

Add the following to 3 plastic zipping bags:
3·¾ c. flour, 1 pkg. dry yeast, 1 t. sugar, ½ t. salt.
Combine well.

Recipe for Homemade ★ DOUGH ★

To 1 bag of dough mix (left), add 1·½ c. very warm water & 2 T. oil. Stir well 'til dough forms. Knead dough on lightly-floured surface for 5 minutes ~ cover & rest 10 minutes. Divide dough in half ~ place in 2 lightly-oiled 12" pizza pans. Let rise 30 minutes in warm place. Bake at 425° for 10 minutes. Remove from oven, cover with sauce & toppings ~ cook 10 more minutes in 425° oven.

PATCHWORK BEAN SOUP MIX

This colorful soup mix would be great paired with crazy quilt potholders or oven mitts!

1/2 c. dried kidney beans
1/2 c. dried black-eyed peas
1/2 c. dried black beans
1/2 c. dried red beans
1/2 c dried split green peas
1/2 c. dried Great Northern beans
1/2 c. dried kidney beans
1/2 c. dried lima beans
3 T. chicken bouillon
1 T. dried, minced onion
salt and pepper to taste
1/2 t. garlic powder
1 T. dried parsley flakes
1 t. celery seeds
1/4 c. brown sugar, packed

Layer each type of bean in a one-quart jar. In a plastic zipping bag, blend together seasonings. For gift giving, attach the following instructions: Add beans to a large stockpot; cover with hot water and let soak overnight. Drain and add 2 quarts of water. Bring to a boil; reduce heat and simmer, covered, one to 2 hours or until beans are almost tender. Stir in two 14 1/2-ounce cans stewed tomatoes and seasoning mix. Simmer, uncovered, one to 1 1/2 hours or until beans are tender. Makes approximately 12 cups of soup.

Amy Butcher
Columbus, GA

Friends will love to get this colorfully layered Patchwork Bean Soup Mix. Instructions for the quilted country potholder and handmade recipe card are on page 132.

Soup mixes don't need to be layered in a jar if you're short on time. Give the mix in a no-sew bag for an easy and welcome gift!

BROWN SUGAR ROUNDS MIX

Delightful with a cup of chamomile tea.

1 1/2 c. all-purpose flour
1/2 t. baking soda
1/4 t. salt
1 1/4 c. brown sugar, packed and divided
1/2 c. chopped pecans

In a large bowl, blend together flour, baking soda and salt. Divide mixture in half and press approximately 1 1/4 cups into the bottom of a one-quart wide-mouth canning jar. Press down firmly so all ingredients will fit inside. Measure out 1/2 cup plus 2 tablespoons brown sugar and layer over flour mixture; pack down well. Add pecans, then layer on remaining brown sugar, packing tightly. Top with remaining flour mixture, pressing down until mixture fits completely into jar. Add a gift tag with the following instructions: Beat together 1/2 cup shortening and 1/2 cup butter until creamy. Add in jar mixture, stirring with a spoon until well blended. Beat together one egg and one teaspoon vanilla extract; stir into flour mixture. Shape dough in two, 10-inch rolls. Wrap in wax paper and chill for 48 hours. When ready to bake, slice cookies 1/4-inch thickness and place on an ungreased baking sheet. Bake at 375 degrees for 10 minutes or until firm. Make approximately 6 dozen cookies.

Kerry Mayer
Denham Springs, LA

White Chocolate Cocoa Mix

a recipe from Marian Buckley
— Fontana, CA —

1 t. vanilla powder
1 t. dried orange zest
½ c. white chocolate chips

Mix ingredients well and store in an airtight container or ½ pint glass canning jar.

✷ Slip a mitten over the top of the jar and pin this instruction tag on the mitten ... a charming little gift!

WHITE CHOCOLATE COCOA

1 ½ c. MILK
¼ c. COCOA MIX

Heat milk in saucepan, then blend in cocoa mix. Stir 'til chocolate chips melt. Serves 2.

Christmas Favorites

Kate, Holly & Mary Elizabeth have gathered this collection of hearty Christmas fare to help you season the holidays with the rich aromas and flavors of farmstyle cooking. Whether you're looking for a quick & easy dish for an office potluck, some delectable sweets to share with neighbors (or to nibble on yourself!) or the fixings for a fabulous family feast, you'll find lots of yummy choices among the savory, time-tested recipes that follow.

Honey-Roasted Pork Loin and Harvest Dressing are just a few of the delicious dishes on the menu for this country Christmas dinner. The easy-to-follow recipes begin on page 96.

let the munching begin!
Holiday Appetizers

Good food and good friends are special blessings we enjoy throughout the holidays. Whether you're hosting a gathering at your home or going to a friend's, you'll make a tasteful addition with one of the scrumptious appetizers in this handy collection. From a festive Patchwork Wheel of Brie to Sausage Stars and BLT Dip, each of our recipes is sure to be a hit. Most can even be made ahead of time, so there's more time to celebrate.

Mixed Fruit Ball, White Christmas Punch

MIXED FRUIT BALL

I like to make a pretty holiday presentation by surrounding this with clusters of red and green grapes and wedges of unpeeled apples.

2 8-oz. pkgs. cream cheese, softened
¼ lb. Cheddar cheese, shredded
1 t. coriander
¼ c. raisins, diced
¼ c. dried apricots, diced
¼ c. dried dates, diced
¼ c. dried prunes, diced
1 c. chopped pecans

Mix cream cheese, Cheddar cheese and coriander until well blended. Add dried fruits and stir gently. Shape into a ball and roll in pecans. Refrigerate overnight.

Jane Williams
Austin, MN

WHITE CHRISTMAS PUNCH

Add a sprinkle of sliced almonds on top of each serving!

2 c. sugar
1 c. water
12-oz. can evaporated milk
1 T. almond extract
6 2-ltr. bottles lemon-lime carbonated drink
3 ½-gal. cartons vanilla ice cream

In a saucepan, combine sugar and water. Stir constantly over medium heat until sugar dissolves. Remove from heat. Add evaporated milk and almond extract; let cool. Chill until ready to serve. Combine milk mixture and lemon-lime drink in punch bowl just before serving. Add ice cream; stir to break ice cream into small pieces.

Rebecca Boone
Olathe, KS

MUSHROOM TURNOVERS

A delicious appetizer to make ahead and freeze.

Crust:
8-oz. pkg. cream cheese
1 c. margarine, softened
2 c. all-purpose flour

Blend together and chill.

Filling:
4 c. sliced mushrooms,
    finely chopped
2/3 c. green onions, chopped
2 T. margarine, melted
1/3 c. sour cream
2 T. all-purpose flour
1/4 t. thyme
1/4 t. salt
1 egg white, beaten
sesame seeds

Sauté mushrooms and onions in margarine for about 3 minutes. Add next 4 ingredients, cooking for a few more minutes. Roll out half of dough at a time to 1/8-inch thickness and cut with a 2 1/2-inch biscuit cutter or a round cookie cutter. Place a heaping 1/4 teaspoon of mushroom mixture in the center of each circle. Fold over and press edges gently with fingers. Transfer turnovers to a lightly greased baking sheet using a spatula; finish sealing edges by pressing with a fork. Brush each turnover with egg white and sprinkle with sesame seeds. Bake at 350 degrees for 20 minutes. Makes about 65 turnovers.

Judy Borecky
Escondido, CA

CRANBERRY-ALMOND PUNCH

A refreshing and colorful punch.

16-oz. can jellied
    cranberry sauce
2 1/4 c. water
3/4 c. orange juice
1/2 c. lemon juice
1 t. almond extract
1 c. chilled ginger ale
Garnish: lemon slices and
    cranberries

With fork, crush cranberry sauce; beat until smooth with hand beater. Beat in water, orange juice, lemon juice and almond extract; chill. At serving time, stir in ginger ale. Garnish each serving with lemon slices and cranberries. Serves 4.

Susan Kennedy
Gooseberry Patch

Brown sugar B·I·T·e·s

a recipe from Barbara Briner ★ San Antonio, Tx

16-oz. pkg. bacon
1 lb. pkg. 2-inch smoked sausages
1/4 c. brown sugar, packed

—

Cut bacon into thirds. Wrap each sausage with a third of a slice of bacon and secure with a toothpick. Place in a baking dish in a single layer. Sprinkle with brown sugar. Bake for 35 to 45 minutes at 375 degrees. Serve warm. Makes about 48.

Mushroom Turnovers, Cranberry-Almond Punch

Cheesy stuffed MUSHROOMS

STUFF YOUR SELF!

a recipe from Sherry Barnhart * Portland, OR

20 to 25 lg. white mushrooms, with stems
2 T. butter
8-oz. pkg. Cheddar cheese, shredded

8-oz. pkg. cream cheese
garlic salt to taste
onion salt to taste
paprika to taste

Carefully remove mushroom stems. Dice stems & sauté them in butter until tender. Set aside to cool. Mix together Cheddar cheese & cream cheese until whipped. Season with garlic salt, onion salt & fold in the stems. Stuff mushrooms & place on a cookie sheet. Sprinkle tops with additional shredded cheese & paprika. Bake at 350 degrees for 15 to 20 minutes or 'til cheese is melted. Serve warm. Makes 20 to 25.

SONIA'S HOLIDAY SANGRIA

Use your favorite fresh fruit in this holiday treat!

1 qt. burgundy wine
2 c. lemon-lime carbonated drink
6-oz. can strawberry nectar
6-oz. can frozen orange juice
6-oz. can peach nectar
1/8 t. cinnamon
1 c. fruit, sliced

Combine all ingredients in a large container, adding fruit last so it will float on top. Cover and refrigerate for 24 hours, allowing flavors to blend. Serve chilled. Makes about 9 cups.

Sonia Bracamonte
Tucson, AZ

PATCHWORK WHEEL OF BRIE

A festive centerpiece for your appetizer table.

5 lb. round of Brie
1/2 c. sweetened dried cranberries or dried currants
1/2 c. walnuts, finely chopped
1/2 c. fresh dill, chopped
1/4 c. poppy seeds
1 c. sliced almonds, toasted

Remove the rind from the top of the cheese by cutting carefully with a sharp knife. Lightly score the top of the cheese into 10 equal pie-shaped sections. Sprinkle half of each of the toppings onto each wedge and press gently until you have decorated all 10 sections. Allow to stand at room temperature for at least 40 minutes before serving. Serve with water crackers or other light wafers. Serves 20 to 25.

Patchwork Wheel of Brie, Sonia's Holiday Sangria

SAUSAGE STARS

This is one of my favorite appetizers. To save time, I make the filling ahead and before serving, fill the wrappers and bake!

4 to 5 doz. won ton wrappers
1 lb. sausage, cooked and crumbled
1½ c. sharp Cheddar cheese, shredded
1½ c. Monterey Jack cheese, shredded
1 c. ranch-style salad dressing
½ c. sweet red pepper, chopped
2¼-oz. can sliced black olives

Press one won ton wrapper in each cup of a muffin tin; bake at 350 degrees for 5 minutes. Remove won tons and place on a baking sheet. Repeat with remaining won tons; set aside. Combine remaining ingredients well and fill baked wrappers. Bake at 350 degrees for an additional 5 minutes or until bubbly. Makes 4 to 5 dozen.

Geri Peterson
Pleasanton, CA

BLT DIP

Serve this with an assortment of crackers or sourdough rounds.

2 c. mayonnaise-style salad dressing
1 c. sour cream
2 lbs. bacon, crisply cooked and crumbled
1 tomato, chopped
2 green onions, chopped

Combine salad dressing and sour cream until well blended. Add bacon and refrigerate overnight. Fold in remaining ingredients.

Sandy Brinkmeier
Lena, IL

CHILI CON QUESO DIP

Serve with tortilla chips, crisp cold veggies and baked pita slices.

28-oz. can plum tomatoes, drained and chopped
2 4-oz. cans green chilies, drained and seeded
1 c. whipping cream
1 lb. Cheddar cheese, shredded
salt and pepper to taste

Over low heat, cook the tomatoes and chilies for about 15 minutes. Stirring constantly, add cream and cheese and continue cooking until mixture thickens. Season with salt and pepper and serve warm.

BROCCOLI & CHEESE HAM ROLLS

This recipe worked well for me served as a brunch for several people. I made the rolls a day ahead and poured the mixture on just before baking. I served fresh fruit and sweet rolls alongside.

2 10-oz. pkgs. frozen, chopped broccoli
8 slices Swiss cheese
8 slices cooked ham
10¾-oz. can mushroom soup
½ c. sour cream
1 t. mustard

Cook broccoli according to package directions; let cool. Place a slice of cheese on a slice of ham. Divide broccoli between the 8 ham-cheese slices. Roll slices and place, seam side down, in a buttered 13"x9" baking dish. Pour mixture of soup, sour cream and mustard over ham rolls. Bake, uncovered, at 350 degrees for 20 minutes.

Cheryl Ewer
Bismarck, ND

MARY ELIZABETH'S crabmeat spread

6½-oz. can crabmeat
8-oz. pkg. cream cheese, softened
⅛ t. salt
¼ t. curry powder
¼ c. green onion, finely chopped
¼ c. green pepper, finely chopped
2 t. lemon juice
½ t. Worchestershire sauce
½ c. sour cream
1 bottle cocktail sauce
crackers

Rinse & remove cartilage from crabmeat. Refrigerate 'til serving. Combine cream cheese, salt, curry powder, onion, pepper, lemon juice, Worchestershire sauce & sour cream in mixing bowl at low speed with mixer 'til well blended. Spread mixture in a shallow dish ~ refrigerate at least 1 hour. Just before serving, pour cocktail sauce over cream cheese mixture & top with crabmeat.
Serve w/crackers.

Softened cream cheese is perfect for piping into cherry tomatoes and pea pods, or onto celery sticks. Garnish with a dash of paprika.

BARBEQUE MEATBALLS

This recipe was given to me by my mother, Nancy Campbell, and is a great appetizer or potluck dish...there are never any left over!

1 lb. ground beef
1/3 c. fine bread crumbs
1 egg, slightly beaten
1/2 t. poultry seasoning
1/2 c. catsup
2 T. brown sugar, packed
2 T. vinegar
2 T. soy sauce

Mix ground beef, bread crumbs, egg and poultry seasoning. Shape into about 2 dozen 1½-inch balls. Brown balls slowly in a lightly oiled skillet over medium-high heat; pour off excess fat. In a small bowl, combine catsup, brown sugar, vinegar and soy sauce. Pour over meatballs. Cover and simmer over low heat, stirring constantly, for 15 minutes. Serve warm.

Suzanne Carbaugh
Mount Vernon, WA

Barbeque Meatballs

HOT MULLED PUNCH

During the holiday season, you will always find some of this punch brewing. It smells wonderful and tastes even better!

1½ qts. cranberry juice
2 qts. apple juice
1/2 c. brown sugar, packed
4 cinnamon sticks, broken
1/2 t. salt
1½ t. whole cloves

Pour juices into 30 to 36-cup coffee maker. Place remaining ingredients in basket of coffee maker and brew according to coffee maker instructions. When complete, remove basket and discard spices. Serve hot. Makes 28 punch cup servings.

Michelle Urdahl
Litchfield, MN

BAGEL CRISPS

Keep in an airtight container to have on hand for snacking during the holidays.

8 bagels, slightly frozen
6 T. margarine
3 t. dried oregano leaves or
    1½ t. garlic powder

Slice the slightly frozen bagels 1/4-inch thick. Lightly butter and sprinkle with oregano or garlic powder. Bake at 250 degrees for 15 to 25 minutes or until crisp.

Peggy Gerch
Lincoln, NE

"The true essentials of a feast are only fun and feed."
— *Oliver Wendell Holmes*

¡Olé! A Spectacular Beginning!
Mexi·Chicken ROLL·UPS

a recipe from Joanne McDonald ★ British Columbia, Canada

8-oz. pkg. cream cheese
1 c. chicken, cooked & chopped
1 c. Monterey Jack cheese, shredded
⅓ c. red pepper, finely chopped

¼ c. fresh coriander
2 T. jalapeño pepper, chopped
2 t. cumin
4 10-inch flour tortillas
Garnish: salsa & sour cream

In a large bowl, combine cream cheese, chicken, cheese, red pepper, coriander, jalapeños & cumin. Spread mixture over tortillas. Roll up tightly. Slice into ½-inch pieces. Bake at 350 degrees for 10 to 15 minutes on lightly oiled baking sheet. Serve with salsa & sour cream. Makes 5 to 6 dozen.

Caponata

For a thoughtful party favor, write guests' names on glass Christmas balls with a gold or silver glitter pen.

CAPONATA

This rich, savory relish will keep for weeks in your refrigerator, if there's any left over!

2 eggplants, peeled
½ c. olive oil
2 onions, sliced
14½-oz. can tomatoes, drained and chopped
1 c. celery, chopped
¼ c. vinegar
2 T. sugar
salt and pepper to taste
¼ c. green olives, chopped
capers to taste

Slice eggplant and squeeze dry with paper towels. Dice into one-inch cubes. Brown in hot oil 10 minutes or until soft and brown, adding onions during last 3 minutes of browning. Add tomatoes and celery; simmer for 15 minutes. Add vinegar, sugar, salt, pepper, olives and capers. Simmer 20 minutes longer over low heat. Tastes best when served at room temperature on crackers or crusty Italian bread.

Santa's SNACK TIME!

Host a homestyle feast this Christmas! From soup to side dishes and dessert, these mouth-watering recipes will invite your family to linger and ask for extra helpings.

HERBED CELERY SOUP
A soup that's a terrific change of pace.

1/4 c. butter
4 c. celery, finely chopped
2 t. dried chives
1 1/2 t. dried tarragon
1/2 t. dried chervil
8 c. chicken broth
1/4 t. sugar
salt and pepper to taste
Garnish: fresh chives

In a medium saucepan, add butter, celery, chives, tarragon and chervil. Cover and cook for 5 minutes or until celery has softened. Add the chicken broth, sugar, salt and pepper; simmer over low heat for 20 minutes. Garnish with fresh chives. Makes about 9 cups.

Kathy Wyatt
Concord, CA

Herbed Celery Soup, Cheddar Shortbread

CHEDDAR SHORTBREAD
For a tasty variation, add sun-dried tomatoes and minced garlic.

2 c. sharp Cheddar cheese, shredded
1 1/2 c. all-purpose flour
3/4 t. dry mustard
1/4 t. salt
1/4 t. cayenne pepper
1/2 c. butter, melted
1 to 2 T. water, optional

Toss first 5 ingredients together; mix in butter. Mix with your hands to form a dough. Add water if dough feels too dry. On a floured surface, roll out half the dough to 1/4-inch thickness. Cut with a 2 1/2-inch star-shaped cookie cutter and place on an ungreased baking sheet. Repeat with the remaining dough. Bake at 375 degrees for 10 to 12 minutes. Remove to rack to cool. Makes 2 dozen.

Robin Sager
Hardin, KY

CORN CHOWDER

I make this soup with the last picking of corn from the garden, but it's just as good with frozen corn!

1 onion, chopped
2 T. butter
2 c. potatoes, diced
1 c. hot water
2 c. milk
2 T. all-purpose flour
10-oz. pkg. frozen whole kernel
    corn
1 t. salt
1/8 t. pepper
Garnish: fresh parsley, chopped

Sauté onion in butter until golden. Add potatoes and hot water; bring to a boil. Cover, reduce heat and simmer until potatoes are tender. Gradually stir milk into flour. Add to potatoes along with corn, salt and pepper. Bring to a boil. Reduce heat; stirring occasionally, simmer about 10 minutes. Garnish with parsley.

Barbara Bargdill
Gooseberry Patch

ALMOND PINE CONES

These cheese balls look so festive on your holiday table.

2 c. whole almonds
12 oz. cream cheese
1/2 c. mayonnaise
5 slices bacon, crisply cooked and
    crumbled
1 t. green onion, finely chopped
1/2 t. dried dill weed
1/8 t. pepper
Garnish: fresh rosemary sprigs

Spread almonds, in a single layer, in a shallow pan. Bake at 300 degrees for 15 minutes, stirring often, until almonds begin to turn color. Combine cream cheese and mayonnaise; mix well. Add bacon, onion, dill and pepper; mix well. Chill overnight. On a serving platter, form cheese mixture into 2 pine cone shapes. Beginning at narrow end, press almonds at slight angle into the cheese mixture in rows. Continue overlapping rows until all cheese is covered. Garnish with fresh rosemary. Serve with crackers.

Laurie Keep
Medina, OH

BACON TREATS

This is always a crowd pleaser.

1 lb. sliced bacon
8-oz. can water chestnuts
1/2 c. mayonnaise-type salad
    dressing
1 c. brown sugar, packed
1/2 c. chili sauce

Slice bacon and water chestnuts in half. Wrap water chestnut with a slice of bacon; secure with a toothpick. Place in a 13"x9" baking dish. Mix all other ingredients together; pour over water chestnuts. Bake at 350 degrees for 45 minutes.

Marsha Downs
Ypsilanti, MI

MARINATED MUSHROOMS

This lightly seasoned salad gives color to your plate without competing with other dominant flavors.

1/2 lb. mushrooms, halved
12 cherry tomatoes
1/2 c. oil-free sweet and sour
    dressing
1 T. fresh parsley, minced

In medium bowl, combine all ingredients. Cover and refrigerate several hours or overnight. Makes 4 servings.

Amy Schueddig
Imperial, MO

Grease the lip of your cream pitcher with butter at that holiday gathering...it will prevent gravy from dripping all over your favorite tablecloth, and it will be easier to clean up for you!

Almond Pine Cones

THREE ♥ FRIENDS
THREE
Layer
RUBY RED SALAD
...PERFECT FOR THE HOLIDAYS!

BOTTOM LAYER:

3-oz. package raspberry gelatin
1 c. boiling water
10-oz. package frozen raspberries in syrup

Dissolve gelatin in boiling water. Add frozen berries and stir until thawed & separated. Pour into a lightly oiled 9" square pan. Place in refrigerator for gelatin to thicken.

Middle LAYER:

1 c. sour cream
3-oz. package cream cheese, softened
2 T. sugar
1/2 c. pecans, chopped

Mix all ingredients together and carefully spread on top of thickened raspberry gelatin. Chill.

Top LAYER:

3-oz. package cherry gelatin
1 c. boiling water
8¼-oz. can crushed pineapple, drained
16-oz. can whole-berry cranberry sauce

Dissolve cherry gelatin in boiling water. Stir in drained pineapple and cranberry sauce. Allow to thicken slightly at room temperature. Carefully spoon over sour cream mixture. Chill until firm. Cut into squares and serve on spinach or lettuce leaves. Garnish with a dollop of whipped cream and a fresh raspberry.

BETTER a GOOD DINNER than a Fine coat. — French Proverb

Each year, for our Christmas dinner table, we put a special favor at each person's place that they get to keep. Usually it's a handmade ornament for the tree.

— Jan Ertola

SALMON WITH DILL SAUCE
This salmon tastes best when served warm or at room temperature.

2 to 3-lb. salmon fillet
1/2 c. soy sauce
1 t. pepper

Dill Sauce:
1/2 c. whipping cream
1/4 c. water
1/4 c. olive oil
1/2 c. brown mustard
1/2 c. fresh dill weed, chopped
4 t. sugar

To prepare salmon, rinse and pat dry. Place, skin side down, on aluminum foil-lined pan and rub with soy sauce. Season with pepper and broil for 12 to 15 minutes. To prepare dill sauce, whisk all ingredients together. To serve, pour sauce over individual servings of salmon.

WILD RICE CASSEROLE
A warm and hearty side dish.

1 to 1¼ c. wild rice, uncooked
1 T. salt
1/2 c. butter
1 onion, finely chopped
1 lb. sliced mushrooms
1/2 c. slivered almonds
1 c. chicken broth
Garnish: sliced almonds

Place rice in a saucepan, adding enough water to cover; soak overnight. When ready to prepare, add salt to rice and water; simmer for 45 to 50 minutes. Drain rice and sauté in butter with onion and mushrooms until onion is soft, but not brown. Mix cooked rice mixture, almonds and chicken broth in a large casserole dish. Cover tightly and cook at 325 degrees for one hour. If it starts to dry out, add more broth. Garnish with sliced almonds.

Mickey Johnson

HONEY-ROASTED PORK LOIN

A wonderful, old-fashioned main dish when served with homemade stuffing or noodles.

2 to 3-lb. boneless pork loin roast
1/4 c. honey
2 T. Dijon mustard
2 T. mixed or black peppercorns,
   crushed
1/2 t. dried thyme
1/2 t. salt

Place roast on a lightly greased rack in a shallow roasting pan. Combine honey and remaining ingredients; brush half of mixture over roast. Bake at 325 degrees for one hour; brush with remaining honey mixture. Bake 30 additional minutes or until thermometer inserted in thickest portion registers 160 degrees.

Sultana Purpora
Englewood, OH

HARVEST DRESSING

Not your ordinary dressing...delicious with pork or poultry!

2 apples, cored and chopped
1/2 c. golden raisins
3 T. butter
1/2 c. walnuts or pecans, coarsely
   chopped
1/4 c. brown sugar, packed
2 c. whole-wheat bread, cubed
apple juice or cider

Sauté apples and raisins in butter; add nuts, brown sugar and bread cubes. Add enough juice to moisten to desired texture. Bake in a 2-quart casserole dish at 400 degrees for 20 to 30 minutes.

Linda Lockwood
St. Louis, MO

Honey-Roasted Pork Loin, Harvest Dressing

PILGRIM SAUCE

A long-time favorite at our home.

1 c. frozen cranberry juice
   concentrate, thawed
1/3 c. sugar
12-oz. pkg. cranberries
1/2 c. dried cranberries
3 T. orange marmalade
2 T. orange juice
2 t. orange zest
1/4 t. allspice

Combine cranberry juice concentrate and sugar in saucepan. Boil, stirring constantly, until sugar dissolves. Add cranberries and cook for about 7 minutes or until fresh berries pop and dried berries soften. Remove from heat; stir in orange marmalade, orange juice, orange zest and allspice. Chill until ready to serve.

Barbara Etzweiler
Millersburg, PA

ASPARAGUS & TOMATO SALAD

This salad has a tasty combination of flavors.

16 stalks asparagus
1 lb. Roma tomatoes, diced
1¹/₂ T. fresh basil, chopped
1 t. salt
¹/₂ t. pepper
¹/₂ lb. Feta cheese, crumbled
¹/₃ c. balsamic vinegar

Cut the stems from asparagus stalks; discard. Slice asparagus on the diagonal and blanch in boiling water for 5 minutes. Remove from boiling water and immediately immerse in cold water to stop the cooking. In a large serving bowl, combine asparagus and tomatoes. Add basil, salt and pepper. Stir in Feta cheese; toss and refrigerate. Before serving, toss with balsamic vinegar.

Barbara Rannazzisi
Elk Grove, CA

"It's a lovely thing...everyone sitting down together, sharing food."

— Alice May Brock

Asparagus & Tomato Salad, Vanilla-Glazed Sweet Potatoes

VANILLA-GLAZED SWEET POTATOES

This heavenly dish is always on our holiday table! It is rich, delicious and there are never any leftovers.

3 lbs. sweet potatoes, peeled
¹/₄ c. butter
¹/₄ c. brown sugar, packed
3 T. orange juice
1 T. vanilla extract
1 t. salt
1 t. orange zest
¹/₄ t. pepper
¹/₂ c. chopped pecans

Boil sweet potatoes in water until tender; drain. Cool slightly, then cut into ¹/₄-inch slices. Arrange the slices in a greased, broiler-proof 13"x9" baking dish, overlapping slightly. In a small saucepan, melt butter over low heat. Add brown sugar, orange juice, vanilla, salt, orange zest and pepper, stirring until combined. Heat, but do not allow to boil. Remove from heat and brush sauce evenly over potato slices. Broil 6 inches from heat until golden, about 6 or 7 minutes. Sprinkle with pecans. Makes 6 servings.

Teri Lindquist
Gurnee, IL

"We hath no better thing to eat under the sun than these mashed potatoes." —Kate

Savory Mashed Potatoes

5 large potatoes, peeled & diced
1/4 c. milk
1/2 t. seasoned salt
3 T. margarine
1 c. sour cream

3-oz. package cream cheese, softened
1 t. dried chives
1/2 c. butter-flavored crackers, crushed
1/4 c. cheddar cheese, shredded

Cook potatoes in salted water 'til tender ~ drain. Beat potatoes, milk, seasoned salt & 2 tablespoons margarine in a mixing bowl until fluffy.

Mix in sour cream, cream cheese & chives. Turn into buttered casserole dish. Combine remaining tablespoon of margarine with crushed cracker crumbs ~ sprinkle on top of potato mixture. Bake for 30 minutes in a 350° oven. Top with shredded cheese during last 10 minutes of baking time. ~Serves 5.

(This recipe can be prepared a day in advance if you wish.)

BAKED BROCCOLI

You can add sliced water chestnuts if you want a little more crunch...very good.

1/2 c. celery, chopped
1/2 c. onion, chopped
2 T. butter
10-oz. pkg. frozen, chopped broccoli
2 c. rice, cooked
10 3/4-oz. can cream of chicken soup
8-oz. jar pasteurized process cheese sauce
1/2 c. milk
1/4 c. bread crumbs, buttered

Sauté celery and onion in butter. Add broccoli and stir until broken up and slightly cooked. Mix together remaining ingredients, except bread crumbs, in a separate bowl. Add to broccoli mixture. Place in a casserole dish coated with non-stick vegetable spray. Cover with buttered crumbs. Bake at 350 degrees for 20 to 30 minutes.

Judy Borecky
Escondido, CA

GOLDEN BUTTER ROLLS

I'm very blessed to have a wonderful mom, and doubly blessed that she's also a great cook. This recipe may seem like a lot of work, but it's well worth the effort. Our entire family loves these delicious rolls!

1 c. milk
1/2 c. butter
1 pkg. active dry yeast
1/2 c. plus 1 t. sugar, divided
1/2 c. lukewarm water
1 t. salt
3 eggs, beaten
1 c. whole-wheat flour
3 1/2 to 4 cups all-purpose flour
3/4 c. butter, softened and divided

In a heavy saucepan, scald milk and butter. Remove from heat and cool. In a small bowl, dissolve yeast and one teaspoon sugar in lukewarm water. When mixture foams, add to a large mixing bowl with remaining sugar, salt, eggs, whole-wheat and all-purpose flour. Add the cooled milk mixture and blend until smooth. Knead on a lightly floured board until shiny, then place in a large oiled bowl; brush the top of dough with 1/4 cup softened butter. Cover and let dough rise until double in size. Divide dough into 3 portions. Using a rolling pin, roll each portion in a 1/2-inch-thick circle. Cut each circle into 10 or 12 pie-shaped wedges. Roll each up from the large end and place one inch apart on a greased baking sheet. Repeat with remaining portions of dough. Brush the tops of each roll with 1/4 cup softened butter; let rise until double. Bake at 375 degrees for 15 to 20 minutes or until golden. Remove and brush with remaining butter while rolls are still warm.

Susan Ingersoll
Gooseberry Patch

RICE PUDDING

This old-fashioned side dish brings back memories of the love and laughter shared at my grandparents' house. Their home was always filled with the sights and smells of many old favorite Swedish dishes.

1/2 c. long-grain rice, uncooked
6 c. milk, divided
1/4 t. salt
3 eggs, beaten
1/3 c. sugar
1 t. vanilla extract
1 c. raisins
Garnish: nutmeg

Rinse rice well; set aside. Scald 4 cups milk, skim off foam and add rice. Add salt and cook over medium heat until mixture thickens, stirring constantly. Add eggs, sugar, vanilla and remaining milk. Stir in raisins; mix well. Transfer mixture to a greased 2-quart casserole dish; sprinkle with nutmeg. Bake at 325 degrees for one hour. Serves 8 to 10.

Janice Carpentier
Aurora, IL

HOLIDAY HOT FUDGE DESSERT

Serve with vanilla ice cream or whipped cream.

1 c. all-purpose flour
2 t. baking powder
3/4 c. sugar
1/4 t. salt
6 T. cocoa, divided
1/2 c. chopped nuts
1/2 c. milk
2 t. oil
1 t. vanilla extract
1 c. brown sugar, packed
1 1/2 c. hot water
Garnish: whipped cream and peppermint candies, crushed

Mix flour, baking powder, sugar, salt, 2 tablespoons cocoa and nuts. Add milk, oil and vanilla. Spread into an 8"x8" baking pan. Combine brown sugar and remaining cocoa and sprinkle on top of mixture in pan. Pour hot water over entire batter. Do not stir. Bake at 350 degrees for 45 to 50 minutes. Garnish with whipped cream and peppermint candies. Serves 6 to 8.

Kim Dubay
Freeport, ME

PUMPKIN ICE CREAM PIE

A quick and easy pie to make for the holidays.

1/2 gal. vanilla ice cream
1 c. canned pumpkin
1/2 c. brown sugar, packed
1 T. orange juice
1/2 t. ginger
1/4 t. cinnamon
1/4 t. nutmeg
9-inch graham cracker crust
Garnish: whipped cream and cinnamon sticks

Place ice cream in a large bowl; cut up and allow to soften. Mix pumpkin, brown sugar, orange juice, ginger, cinnamon and nutmeg, using an electric mixer. Add to the softened ice cream and mix well. Spoon into graham cracker crust. Freeze until firm. Garnish with whipped cream and whole cinnamon sticks. Serves 8.

Brenda Umphress
Colorado Springs, CO

Rice Pudding, Holiday Hot Fudge Dessert

HOLIDAY FRUITCAKE

There have been lots of jokes about inedible and tasteless fruitcakes that nobody in their right mind would eat, but this fruitcake is always greeted with cheers and devoured.

2½ c. all-purpose flour
1 t. baking soda
2 eggs, beaten
27-oz. jar mincemeat
14-oz. can sweetened condensed
    milk
¼ c. apricot brandy, optional
1 lb. mixed candied fruit
½ lb. red candied cherries
1½ c. walnuts, coarsely chopped
Garnish: walnut halves and
    red and green candied cherries

Sift together flour and baking soda; set aside. Combine eggs, mincemeat, sweetened condensed milk and brandy, if desired. Stir in fruit and nuts. Stir in flour mixture. Turn into three 7³/₈"x3⁵/₈" loaf pans lined with wax paper coated with non-stick vegetable spray. Decorate tops of cakes with walnut halves and red and green candied cherries. Bake at 300 degrees for one hour and 25 minutes or until center springs back when touched and top is golden; cool. Turn out and remove wax paper. When completely cool, wrap in new wax paper and then in aluminum foil. Store in a cool place for up to 6 weeks.

Kathy-Leigh Russo

Can one desire too much of a good thing?
— Shakespeare, "As You Like It"

Pumpkin Ice Cream Pie, Holiday Fruitcake

Sweet Treats

*Crispy, creamy, moist & dreamy…
every delightful morsel of these homemade
holiday treats will melt in your mouth!*

Christmas Morning Almond Pound Cake

CHRISTMAS MORNING ALMOND POUND CAKE

Serve while the presents are being opened, or make it as a gift for a family you love.

2/3 c. butter, softened
8 oz. almond paste
1 t. almond extract
1 t. vanilla extract
1¼ c. sugar
4 eggs
1 t. baking powder
¼ c. sour cream
2½ c. all-purpose flour
¾ c. milk
Garnish: powdered sugar, whipped cream and maraschino cherries with stems

In a bowl, blend together butter, almond paste and extracts until smooth. Slowly add sugar and beat again. Add eggs, one at a time, beating after each addition. Add baking powder to sour cream; beat together and add to above mixture. Slowly add flour alternately with milk until you have a nice smooth batter. Pour into a greased and floured 12-cup Bundt® pan. Bake at 325 degrees for 50 to 55 minutes or until the top is golden brown and it springs back when touched. Turn off oven and open oven door. Let sit about 30 minutes and then remove to counter on rack or cutting board. When cool, remove to a serving dish. Garnish with powdered sugar, dollop of whipped cream and maraschino cherries.

*Wendy Paffenroth
Pine Island, NY*

ALL I WANT FOR CHRISTMAS IS

THIS MINOR LIST OF
INEXPENSIVE WHAT-NOTS AND

CHOCOLATE RAPTURE

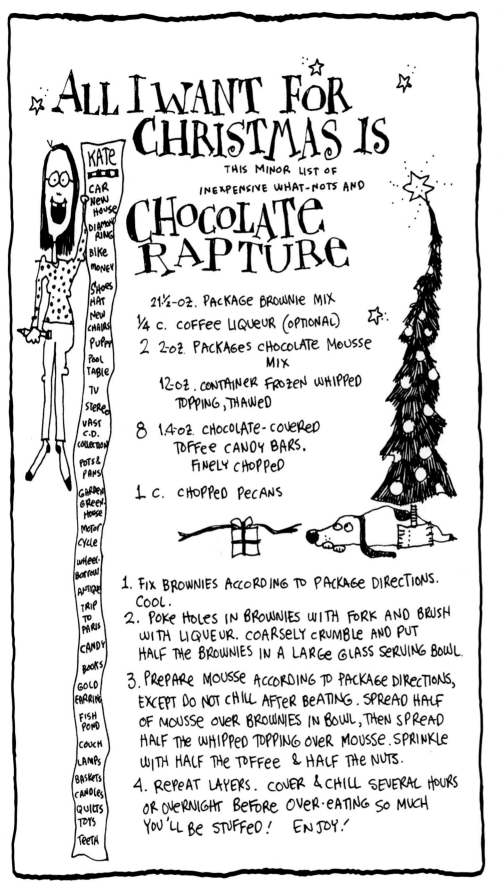

KATE
CAR
NEW HOUSE
DIAMOND RING
BIKE
MONEY
SHOES
HAT
NEW CHAIRS
PUPPY
POOL TABLE
TV
STEREO
VAST C.D. COLLECTION
POTS & PANS
GARDEN GREENHOUSE
MOTOR CYCLE
WHEEL-BORROW
ANTIQUE
TRIP TO PARIS
CANDY
BOOKS
GOLD EARRING
FISH POND
COUCH
LAMPS
BASKETS
CANDLES
QUILTS
TOYS
TEETH

21½-OZ. PACKAGE BROWNIE MIX

¼ C. COFFEE LIQUEUR (OPTIONAL)

2 2-OZ. PACKAGES CHOCOLATE MOUSSE MIX

12-OZ. CONTAINER FROZEN WHIPPED TOPPING, THAWED

8 1.4-OZ. CHOCOLATE-COVERED TOFFEE CANDY BARS, FINELY CHOPPED

1 C. CHOPPED PECANS

1. FIX BROWNIES ACCORDING TO PACKAGE DIRECTIONS. COOL.

2. POKE HOLES IN BROWNIES WITH FORK AND BRUSH WITH LIQUEUR. COARSELY CRUMBLE AND PUT HALF THE BROWNIES IN A LARGE GLASS SERVING BOWL.

3. PREPARE MOUSSE ACCORDING TO PACKAGE DIRECTIONS, EXCEPT DO NOT CHILL AFTER BEATING. SPREAD HALF OF MOUSSE OVER BROWNIES IN BOWL, THEN SPREAD HALF THE WHIPPED TOPPING OVER MOUSSE. SPRINKLE WITH HALF THE TOFFEE & HALF THE NUTS.

4. REPEAT LAYERS. COVER & CHILL SEVERAL HOURS OR OVERNIGHT BEFORE OVER-EATING SO MUCH YOU'LL BE STUFFED! ENJOY!

FONDANT

While I was growing up, our family would begin making candy on the first Sunday afternoon in December and continue each Sunday until Christmas. It was such a wonderful "together" time. Dad always cracked the nuts and my two brothers licked the pans!

2 c. sugar
1 c. milk
2 T. margarine
1 t. vanilla extract
Garnish: pecan halves

Combine sugar and milk in a saucepan and cook to a soft-ball stage or 238 degrees on a candy thermometer. Remove from heat. Add margarine and vanilla; cool. Using a heavy-duty mixer, or kneading by hand, mix until stiff enough to shape into balls. Using approximately one teaspoonful, roll fondant into balls and top each ball with a pecan half. Makes approximately 40 pieces of fondant.

Marjorie Foland
Wilmington, OH

CARAMEL CORN

Great for slumber parties or whenever you have a houseful of munchers!

½ c. margarine
2 c. brown sugar, packed
½ c. corn syrup
½ t. salt
1 t. vanilla extract
1 t. baking soda
6 qts. popped popcorn

Heat margarine, brown sugar, corn syrup and salt until it comes to a boil. Continue to boil for 5 minutes without stirring. Remove from heat. Add vanilla and baking soda; stir. Pour over freshly popped popcorn. Bake one hour at 250 degrees, stirring every 20 minutes.

Judy Borecky
Escondido, CA

ANNIE'S SOFT MOLASSES COOKIES

Madge's aunt used to make these yummy cookies 4 inches in size and bake them in a woodstove!

1 c. sugar
1 c. shortening, melted
1 c. molasses
1 egg, beaten
4 t. baking soda
2/3 c. hot water
1 T. vanilla extract
5 c. all-purpose flour
1 1/2 t. cream of tartar
1 1/2 t. ginger
1 1/2 t. cinnamon
1/2 t. ground cloves
3/4 t. salt
1/2 c. vanilla frosting

Mix sugar, shortening and molasses; add egg. Dissolve baking soda in the hot water and add vanilla; mix well and set aside. Sift together flour, cream of tartar, spices and salt. Add water mixture. Combine thoroughly with molasses mixture. Chill dough for at least 3 hours. Roll out dough to 1/4-inch thickness and cut out with desired 2 3/4-inch cookie cutter. Place on greased baking sheet. Bake at 375 degrees for 7 minutes; let cool. Place frosting in a small microwave-safe bowl; microwave on high for 20 seconds. Stir well. Microwave 5 additional seconds, if needed to make a good dipping consistency. Dip tips of cookies in frosting. Makes about 4 dozen cookies.

Madge Bowman
Shreve, OH

Annie's Soft Molasses Cookies, Cheesecake Cookies

CHOCOLATE-PEANUT BUTTER CUPCAKES

A treat for any celebration! Make them extra special by dusting tops with powdered sugar using lace paper doilies or heart cut-outs.

Filling:
2 T. whipping cream
2 oz. semi-sweet baking
    chocolate, grated
2 t. sugar
1/4 c. creamy peanut butter

Cupcakes:
6 T. butter
6 oz. semi-sweet baking
    chocolate
2 eggs
2/3 c. sugar
1 t. vanilla extract
3/4 c. all-purpose flour
1/4 t. baking soda
1/4 t. salt

To prepare filling, heat cream in small saucepan until boiling. In a mixing bowl, pour cream over chocolate and sugar; stir until combined and chocolate melts. Add peanut butter and mix well. Refrigerate filling for 35 to 40 minutes or until slightly firm. In double boiler over low heat, melt butter and chocolate. In mixing bowl, beat eggs until foamy, adding sugar and vanilla; beat until fluffy. Beating at low speed, add melted chocolate mixture. Beat in flour, baking soda and salt; mix until just combined. Pour batter into muffin tins coated with non-stick vegetable spray, filling 2/3 full. Roll rounded teaspoonfuls of filling and press one ball lightly into the center of each cupcake. Bake at 350 degrees for 15 to 20 minutes.

CHEESECAKE COOKIES

These are my favorite cookies because they're so moist and tasty. I remember they were considered a special treat, usually made for company, but once in awhile we'd come home from school and a pan of them, warm from the oven, would be waiting for us!

1/3 c. butter
1/3 c. brown sugar, packed
1 c. all-purpose flour
1/2 c. walnuts, finely chopped
1/4 c. sugar
8-oz. pkg. cream cheese
1 egg
2 T. milk
1 T. lemon juice
1/2 t. vanilla extract

Cream butter with brown sugar in a small mixing bowl. Add flour and walnuts; blend together. Mixture will be crumbly. Reserve one cup for topping. Press remainder of mixture into the bottom of an 8"x8" baking pan. Bake at 350 degrees for 12 to 15 minutes or until lightly browned. Blend sugar with cream cheese until smooth. Add egg, milk, lemon juice and vanilla; beat well. Spread over baked crust and sprinkle with reserved topping. Bake for 25 minutes. Cool; cut into 2-inch squares.

Mary Walsh
Valencia, CA

ROCKY ROAD FUDGE

★ 4 4½-ounce milk chocolate bars
★ 3 c. miniature marshmallows
★ 3/4 c. coarsely broken walnuts

PARTIALLY MELT CHOCOLATE BARS OVER LOW HEAT IN SMALL PAN. REMOVE FROM HEAT ~ BEAT SMOOTH. STIR IN NUTS & MARSHMALLOWS. LET COOL AND SNARF DIRECTLY FROM PAN ~ OR SPREAD IN BUTTERED 8"x8" PAN, CHILL & CUT WHEN SET.

Now I lay me down to sleep,
a pan of fudge here at my feet;
If I should die before I wake,
you'll know I died of stomach ache.

—COUNTRY FRIENDS' VARIATION OF OLD RHYME

Every year, each of my children selects one old favorite cookie recipe and one new one for us to prepare. It's amazing how favorites change, and how they "remember" who discovered the new favorite.

— Kathy Christianson

WHITE CHOCOLATE MACADAMIA BROWNIE PIE

The crunchy macadamia nuts combine with the creamy white chocolate to create a fabulous taste sensation.

1/2 c. unsalted butter, softened
1 c. sugar
2 eggs
1/2 c. all-purpose flour
1/4 c. cocoa
1 t. vanilla extract
1/2 c. macadamia nuts, chopped
3 oz. white chocolate chips

Cream butter and sugar together and beat in the eggs. Add flour, cocoa and vanilla. Fold in the nuts and chips. Pour into a greased 9" pie pan. Bake at 325 degrees for 35 minutes. Pie should be moist; toothpick will not come out completely clean. Let cool, but serve slightly warm, if possible, with a scoop of vanilla ice cream on the side.

PECAN FINGERS

Using real butter gives these cookies a rich flavor.

1 c. butter, softened
2 c. all-purpose flour
1/2 c. powdered sugar
2 t. vanilla extract
2 c. pecans, finely chopped
Garnish: powdered sugar

Cream butter; mix in flour, powdered sugar and vanilla. Add pecans, mixing well. Chill dough until firm. Roll into finger lengths and place on a greased baking sheet. Bake at 250 degrees for one hour. Roll in powdered sugar while still warm.

Jane Keichinger

THE PEANUT BUTTER BARS

Many years ago when I was in elementary school, our "Lunch Lady," Mrs. Hopkins, made these for us once a week. The aroma filled the school as they were baking and we knew we were in store for the best possible treat. I've never had anything that tasted so good! Now I make these for my own family and they agree...they are THE Peanut Butter Bars.

1¹/₂ c. plus 2 T. butter, softened
³/₄ c. peanut butter
¹/₄ c. corn syrup
1 c. sugar
1³/₄ c. all-purpose flour
2 eggs
1 t. salt

Cream butter and peanut butter; add corn syrup, sugar, flour, eggs and salt. Mix about 5 minutes. Spread in greased 13"x9" baking pan. Bake at 350 degrees for 25 minutes, watching carefully. Cool, ice and cut into squares.

Icing:
¹/₄ c. shortening, melted and cooled
¹/₂ c. cocoa
¹/₄ t. salt
¹/₃ c. milk
1¹/₂ t. vanilla extract
3¹/₂ c. powdered sugar

Combine shortening, cocoa and salt. Add milk and vanilla. Stir in powdered sugar in three parts; beat well.

Carol Bull
Delaware, OH

Mom's Candy Apple Walnut Pie

MOM'S CANDY APPLE WALNUT PIE

The red hots add the spice.

2 frozen 9-inch deep-dish pie crusts
6 c. cooking apples, thinly sliced
²/₃ c. chopped walnuts
¹/₂ c. cinnamon red hot candies
¹/₃ c. plus 2 T. sugar, divided
¹/₃ c. all-purpose flour

If desired, let one pie crust thaw, and reshape edges into a fluted design. Set aside. In a large bowl, toss together apples, walnuts, cinnamon candies, ¹/₃ cup sugar and flour. Pour into fluted pie crust. Break and crumble second frozen crust into very small pieces; toss with remaining 2 tablespoons sugar. Sprinkle over apples. Bake at 375 degrees on a baking sheet for 55 to 60 minutes or until candies melt and bubble up through the crumbled crust. Cool completely before serving. Makes 8 servings.

Juanita Williams
Jacksonville, OR

CRUSTLESS PUMPKIN PIE

A great alternative to pumpkin pie!

16-oz. can pumpkin
12-oz. can evaporated milk
1½ c. sugar
4 eggs
2 t. pumpkin pie spice
1 t. salt
18¼-oz. pkg. yellow cake mix
1 c. chopped nuts
2 sticks butter, melted
Garnish: whipped topping and
nutmeg

Combine pumpkin, milk, sugar, eggs, pumpkin pie spice and salt, blending well. Pour into an ungreased 13"x9" baking dish and sprinkle cake mix over top. Sprinkle on nuts. Drizzle butter onto cake mix; do not stir. Bake at 350 degrees for 45 minutes to an hour, testing for doneness. Serve with whipped topping and a sprinkle of nutmeg.

Linda Webb
Delaware, OH

CINNAMON PUDDING CAKE

A terrific dessert for a chilly winter evening! Serve with a mug of homemade cocoa.

1 c. sugar
2 T. butter, softened
1 c. milk
2 c. all-purpose flour
2 t. baking powder
2 t. cinnamon
¼ t. salt

Mix all ingredients together and blend well. Pour into a greased 13"x9" baking pan; add topping.

Topping:
2 c. brown sugar, packed
2 T. butter
1¼ c. water

Combine all ingredients in a saucepan; bring to a boil. Pour mixture over the cake batter; do not stir. Bake at 350 degrees for 25 minutes. Makes 12 servings.

Phyllis Peters
Three Rivers, MI

Pecan Pie Mini Muffins

a recipe from Kathy Mentink
★ Elgin, IL

1 c. brown sugar, packed
½ c. all-purpose flour
1 c. pecans, chopped
⅔ c. butter, melted
2 eggs, beaten

*

In a bowl, combine first three ingredients; set aside. Combine butter & eggs, mix well. Stir into flour mixture until just moistened. Fill paper-lined miniature muffin cups ⅔ full. Bake at 350 degrees for 20 to 25 minutes or until tested done. Remove immediately to cool on wire racks. Makes 3 dozen muffins.

Crustless Pumpkin Pie, Pecan Pie Mini Muffins

"Nine out of 10 people like chocolate. The tenth person always lies."
— John G. Tullius

No one can resist piping hot, crusty breads and delicious muffins fresh from the oven!

DAMASCUS BRICK SWEET ROLLS

There's nothing like the smell of fresh breads baking to welcome guests. The memories and smells of their childhood soon warm their hearts.

1 c. plus 2 T. milk, divided
1 c. butter, divided
2 t. salt
$\frac{1}{2}$ c. plus 1 t. sugar, divided
2 pkgs. active dry yeast
1 c. warm water
1 egg, beaten
6 to 7 c. bread flour
cinnamon-sugar to taste
2 c. powdered sugar
$\frac{1}{2}$ t. vanilla extract

Combine one cup milk, $\frac{1}{2}$ cup butter, salt and $\frac{1}{2}$ cup sugar in a large saucepan until just warm. In a small mixing bowl, combine yeast and water until yeast is dissolved; add remaining sugar. When yeast mixture begins to foam, add to milk mixture; mix well. Fold in egg. Add flour and knead just until smooth. Roll dough out on a floured surface to a 16"x12" rectangle. Sprinkle with cinnamon-sugar mixture to taste; dot with remaining butter. Roll up dough lengthwise and cut into one-inch slices. Place on a lightly greased baking sheet; cover and let rise 25 minutes or until double. Bake at 375 degrees for 12 to 15 minutes. Combine powdered sugar, remaining milk and vanilla; drizzle over rolls. Makes 1$\frac{1}{2}$ dozen rolls.

The Damascus Brick
Junction City, OH

Damascus Brick Sweet Rolls

MACADAMIA MINI-LOAVES
A delicious coconut-flavored bread.

3 1/2-oz. jar macadamia nuts
1/3 c. flaked coconut
1 1/2 c. plus 1 T. sugar, divided
1 lemon
3/4 c. butter, softened
3 c. all-purpose flour
1/2 c. milk
1 1/2 t. vanilla extract
1 t. baking powder
2 eggs

Finely chop enough macadamia nuts to measure 1/3 cup; set aside. Coarsely chop remaining nuts; place in a small bowl and stir in coconut and one tablespoon sugar. Grate 2 teaspoons lemon zest and squeeze 3 tablespoons juice. Grease and flour four 5 3/4"x3 1/4" loaf pans or one 9" tube pan. In a large bowl, with mixer at high speed, beat butter and remaining sugar until light and fluffy. At low speed, beat in flour, milk, vanilla, baking powder, eggs, lemon zest and juice until just mixed, constantly scraping the bowl. Stir in reserved macadamia nuts. Spoon batter into pans. Sprinkle coconut mixture evenly over batter, then lightly press into batter. Bake small loaves at 350 degrees for 60 minutes or tube cake for one hour 10 minutes or until toothpick inserted in center comes out clean. If topping begins to brown too quickly, loosely cover pans with aluminum foil. Cool cakes in pans on wire racks for 10 minutes; remove from pans. Cool completely on racks. Makes 4 loaves, 4 servings each or 1 ring, 16 servings.

Terri Rasmussen
Orange, CA

Angel Biscuits

Heavenly!

Light and Fluffy!
Make the dough the night before for fresh hot biscuits on Christmas morning!

☆ 2.3/4 c. flour
☆ 2 T. sugar
☆ 1.1/2 t. baking powder
☆ 1/2 t. baking soda
☆ 1/2 t. salt
☆ 1 stick margarine
☆ 2 T. warm water
☆ 1 c. buttermilk
☆ 1 pkg. active dry yeast

Combine flour, sugar, baking powder, baking soda & salt in large mixing bowl. With a pastry blender or 2 knives, cut in margarine until mixture resembles coarse meal. Place yeast in small bowl & dissolve with 2 T. of warm water. Mix dissolved yeast & buttermilk into coarse flour mixture. Do not overmix! Dough should just cling together. Knead dough gently (about 12 strokes) on well-floured surface. Grease a bowl with shortening or oil. Place dough in bowl & cover with plastic wrap. Chill overnight. The next morning, roll dough to 1/2" thickness on floured surface. Cut with a 2-to-3" cookie or biscuit cutter. Place on baking sheet. Cover with clean towel ～ let rise in a warm place for about 30 minutes. Bake for 10 to 12 minutes at 400° or until golden brown. Serve warm with butter & honey. Makes 18-to-24 biscuits.

Bread is the warmest and kindest of words. ～ RUSSIAN SAYING

111

BRAZIL NUT LOAF

Enjoy one loaf and take the other to a party.

1½ c. all-purpose flour
1½ c. sugar
1 t. baking powder
1 t. salt
10-oz. pkg. whole pitted dates
2 c. chopped walnuts
1 c. Brazil nuts
10-oz. jar maraschino cherries, drained
5 eggs, beaten
1 t. vanilla extract

Sift together dry ingredients and add dates, nuts and cherries. Stir to coat with flour mixture. Add eggs and vanilla. Blend everything well. Spoon into two 8½"x4½" greased loaf pans. Bake at 325 degrees for one hour 15 minutes to one hour 20 minutes. Cool.

Judy Borecky
Escondido, CA

EASY ORANGE ROLLS

So easy to make, and what a wonderful aroma while they're baking!

½ c. butter
¾ c. sugar
2 T. frozen orange juice
zest of 2 oranges
3 12-oz. tubes refrigerated biscuits

In a small saucepan, combine butter and sugar. Heat until sugar dissolves. Blend in frozen orange juice and orange zest. Dip individual biscuits in orange mixture and layer in a lightly oiled Bundt® pan; repeat with all biscuits. Pour any remaining orange mixture over biscuits. Bake at 375 degrees for 20 minutes.

Robyn Wright
Delaware, OH

Brazil Nut Loaf

PUMPKIN NUT BREAD

Easy snacking for the Christmas crowd.

3¼ c. all-purpose flour
¾ c. quick-cooking oats, uncooked
2 t. baking soda
1½ t. pumpkin pie spice
½ t. baking powder
½ t. salt
3 eggs
15-oz. can pumpkin
1½ c. sugar
1½ c. brown sugar, packed
½ c. water
½ c. oil
½ c. evaporated milk
1 c. chopped walnuts

Combine flour, oats, baking soda, pumpkin pie spice, baking powder and salt in a large bowl. Beat together eggs, pumpkin, sugars, water, oil and evaporated milk on medium speed until combined. Beat flour mixture into pumpkin mixture until blended; stir in nuts. Fill 2 greased 9"x5" loaf pans and bake at 350 degrees for one hour and 5 minutes to one hour and 10 minutes or until toothpick comes out clean. Cool in pans 10 minutes; remove from pans to cool completely.

CRUSTY CORNMEAL ROLLS

A delicious roll that's worth the time...prepare a good vegetable soup while you're waiting for the dough to rise!

2 c. milk
1/2 c. shortening, melted
1/2 c. sugar
1/3 c. cornmeal
1 1/2 t. salt
2 eggs, beaten
1 pkg. active dry yeast
1/4 c. lukewarm water
4 1/2 to 5 c. all-purpose flour
3 T. butter, melted

In a double boiler, combine milk, shortening, sugar, cornmeal and salt. Stir the mixture often, cooking until thick. Allow to cool; add eggs. Dissolve yeast in water and add to batter. Beat well; cover and let rise in a greased bowl for about 2 hours. After batter has risen, add flour to form a soft dough. Knead dough lightly and let rise again for another hour; knead again. Roll dough out to one-inch thickness with a floured rolling pin and use a 2 1/2-inch biscuit cutter to cut out dough. Brush with butter. Place on a greased baking sheet. Cover and let rise for another hour. Bake at 375 degrees for 13 to 15 minutes or until golden. Makes 20 rolls.

Crusty Cornmeal Rolls, Honeybee Butter

HONEYBEE BUTTER

• 1 STICK BUTTER
• 6 T. HONEY

• Beat ingredients together 'til fluffy.

WHOLE-WHEAT BREAD

A lady in our church has been making this bread for us for more years than I am allowed to mention! It's delicious and easy to make.

3 c. warm water
3 pkgs. active dry yeast
1/4 c. honey
5 c. whole-wheat flour
5 t. salt
5 c. all-purpose flour
5 T. oil

Mix together water, yeast and honey. Add whole-wheat flour and salt; mix well. Stir in all-purpose flour. Pour oil over the dough and knead 2 to 3 minutes. Cover dough and let rise for 45 minutes. Punch down and knead slightly. Shape into 2 loaves and place in 2 greased 9"x5" loaf pans. Let rise until double in size. Bake at 400 degrees for 20 minutes, then loosely cover with a tent of aluminum foil. Bake 10 minutes longer. Makes 2 loaves.

Diann Fox
Lewisberry, PA

DILLY ONION BREAD

An easy-to-make quick bread that's full of flavor!

3 c. all-purpose flour
1/2 c. plus 2 T. sugar
1 1/2 T. baking powder
2/3 c. butter
1 c. milk
4 eggs
5 t. dill seed
2 t. dried, minced onion

Oil four 6-inch loaf pans; set aside. Using a large bowl, combine flour, sugar and baking powder well; cut in butter. In a separate bowl, blend milk, eggs, dill seed and onion. Add to flour mixture and stir. Pour equal amounts into prepared loaf pans and bake at 350 degrees for 30 minutes or until a knife inserted in the center comes out clean. Cool on a rack and serve warm.

Apricot Crescents

APRICOT CRESCENTS

Serve these with a steaming mug of chamomile tea and fresh fruit. Perfect for breakfast or a light brunch.

1 c. butter
2 c. all-purpose flour
1 egg yolk
1/2 c. sour cream
1/2 c. sugar, divided
1/2 c. apricot preserves
1/2 c. flaked coconut
1/4 c. pecans, finely chopped
sugar

Cut butter into flour until mixture resembles coarse crumbs. Beat egg yolk with sour cream; add to crumb mixture and blend well. Divide into fourths; shape into balls and flatten into 1/2-inch thickness between layers of plastic wrap. Chill several hours or overnight. Remove dough from refrigerator and let stand 10 minutes. Combine preserves, coconut and pecans, stirring well. Working with one portion of dough at a time, roll into a 10 1/2-inch circle on a floured surface. Sprinkle with 2 tablespoons sugar. Place 3 tablespoons of filling on circle; gently spread filling over dough with a pastry brush. Cut each circle into 12 pie-shaped wedges and roll into a crescent shape, beginning at the wide end. Sprinkle each rolled crescent with additional sugar. Place one inch apart on greased baking sheet. Repeat with remaining dough, sugar and filling. Bake at 350 degrees for 15 to 17 minutes or until lightly browned. Immediately remove from oven and place on wire racks to cool. Makes 4 dozen.

Rene Smith
Shawnee, OK

OATMEAL APPLE MUFFINS

Muffins with a fresh apple flavor.

1 c. quick-cooking oats, uncooked
3/4 c. milk
1/2 c. raisins, optional
1 1/4 c. all-purpose flour
2 t. baking powder
1/2 t. salt
1/2 t. cinnamon
1 egg
1/2 c. brown sugar, packed
1/4 c. oil
1 to 2 apples, peeled, cored and chopped

In a small bowl, combine oats and milk; set aside. Soak raisins in a little hot water to "plump" them; drain. Combine in a medium bowl, flour, baking powder, salt and cinnamon; mix well. Beat egg, brown sugar and oil until blended. Add egg mixture to dry ingredients; stir until well blended. Stir in oat mixture, apples and raisins. Stir together until blended. Grease and fill muffin tins 3/4 full. Bake at 400 degrees for 15 to 20 minutes.

Kathleen Griffin
N. Charleston, SC

BROWN SUGAR & CINNAMON BUTTER

1 STICK OF BUTTER, SOFTENED
4 t. BROWN SUGAR, PACKED
1/4 t. CINNAMON
1/8 t. NUTMEG
.....
In a small bowl, beat all ingredients together until fluffy.

FIELDSTONE FARM POPOVERS

Our daughter Emily loves these warm from the oven with butter and jam!

2 eggs
1 c. milk
1 c. all-purpose flour
½ t. salt

Butter 8 custard cups and place in oven on a baking sheet while preparing batter. Beat eggs slightly and add remaining ingredients. Beat mixture on medium speed for one minute, scraping sides of bowls. Batter should be smooth and thin. Remove custard cups from oven and fill each custard cup ⅓ full. Bake at 400 degrees for 50 minutes or until crisp and golden-brown. Do not open oven during baking time or popovers may fall.

Vickie

ENGLISH MUFFIN BREAD

The first time I made this bread we ate the whole loaf in one sitting!

2 pkgs. active dry yeast
½ c. warm water
5 c. all-purpose flour, divided
2 t. cinnamon
2 T. sugar
1 t. salt
¼ t. baking soda
1½ c. warm orange juice
¼ c. oil
½ c. chopped walnuts or pecans
½ c. dried apricots, chopped
cornmeal to taste

Dissolve yeast in water; set aside. Combine 2 cups flour, cinnamon, sugar, salt and baking soda; stir in yeast mixture. Blend in orange juice and oil. Beat mixture on low until thoroughly combined. Increase speed to high and blend for an additional 3 minutes. Stir in nuts, apricots and remaining flour to form a stiff batter. Do not knead. Spoon batter into 2 lightly oiled 9"x5" loaf pans; sprinkle cornmeal over tops of loaves. Cover and let rise for 45 minutes. Bake at 350 degrees for 35 to 40 minutes. Makes 2 loaves.

Madge Bowman
Shreve, OH

Come for Brunch

Serve a basket-full!

Holly's Lemon Raspberry Yogurt Muffins

ingredients:
2 eggs, beaten
½ c. milk
½ c. lemon yogurt
4 T. butter, melted
1 t. vanilla
2 c. flour
1 T. baking powder
1 t. salt
1 t. lemon peel, finely grated

⅔ c. sugar
2 c. raspberries

Yields 12 Muffins

Combine eggs, milk, yogurt, butter & vanilla. In a medium bowl, stir together flour, baking powder, salt, lemon peel & sugar. Mix yogurt mixture into dry ingredients. In 2 to 3 strokes, fold in raspberries. Spoon into greased muffin cups. Bake at 350° for 18 to 20 minutes or when top springs back when touched. Serve plain or brush warm muffins with...

Lemon Glaze

2 T. lemon juice   1 t. lemon peel, finely grated
½ c. powdered sugar

Combine ingredients and brush over warm muffins.

"Bread cast upon the waters comes back eclairs."
— Bert Greene

You'll love these nutritious, oh-so-easy dishes for casual holiday meals and potlucks.

NANCY'S TURKEY PIE

A yummy main course that only needs a salad and a simple dessert for a complete meal.

$^1/_2$ c. butter, softened
1 c. sour cream
1 egg
1 c. all-purpose flour
1 t. salt
1 t. baking powder
$^1/_2$ t. dried sage

Combine butter, sour cream and egg. Beat at medium speed until smooth. Add flour, salt, baking powder and sage; blend at low speed, mixing well. Spread batter evenly over the bottom and up the sides of an ungreased 9$^1/_2$" deep-dish pie plate.

Filling:
$^1/_3$ c. carrot, chopped
$^1/_3$ c. onion, chopped
$^1/_3$ c. green pepper, chopped
$^1/_3$ c. celery, chopped
$^1/_3$ c. red pepper, chopped
2 c. cooked turkey, chopped
10$^3/_4$-oz. can cream of chicken
     soup
$^1/_2$ c. Cheddar cheese, shredded

Mix together vegetables, turkey and soup; place into pie crust and sprinkle with Cheddar cheese. Bake at 375 degrees for one hour. Let stand 15 minutes before serving.

Delores Hollenbeck
Omaha, NE

Nancy's Turkey Pie

HEARTY BEEF BRISKET

Slow-cooking makes the meat tender. Let it roast while you wrap packages or trim the tree!

16-oz. can stewed tomatoes, chopped
8-oz. can sauerkraut
1 c. applesauce
2 T. brown sugar, packed
3½ lb. beef brisket
2 T. cold water
2 T. cornstarch

Combine tomatoes, sauerkraut, applesauce and brown sugar in a Dutch oven. Bring to a boil; then reduce heat. Add brisket, spooning tomato mixture over top; cover and simmer on low 2 to 3 hours or until meat is tender. When brisket is thoroughly cooked, remove from Dutch oven and set aside. In a small bowl, combine cold water and cornstarch, whisking well. Blend into tomato mixture in Dutch oven. Cook until mixture thickens; continue to cook for 2 additional minutes. Spread sauce over top of brisket, reserving some as gravy.

Joanne West
Beavercreek, OH

SPINACH PIE

This is a terrific, light meal I like to serve with muffins and fresh fruit.

16-oz. carton cottage cheese
10-oz. pkg. frozen chopped spinach, thawed and drained
8 oz. Cheddar cheese, shredded
3 eggs, beaten
¼ c. butter, melted
3 T. all-purpose flour
salt blend to taste

Combine all ingredients. Pour into a 9" pie pan. Bake at 325 degrees for one hour. Cool slightly and cut into wedges.

Nancy Burton
Wamego, KS

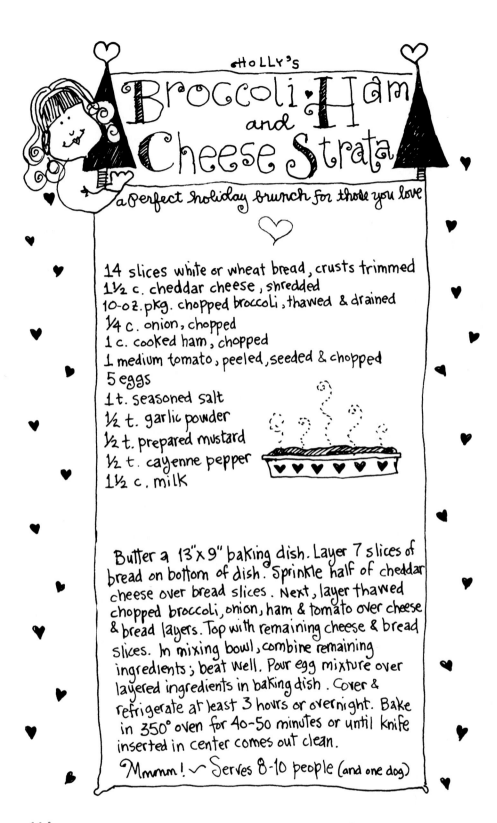

Holly's Broccoli Ham and Cheese Strata

a perfect holiday brunch for those you love

14 slices white or wheat bread, crusts trimmed
1½ c. cheddar cheese, shredded
10-oz. pkg. chopped broccoli, thawed & drained
¼ c. onion, chopped
1 c. cooked ham, chopped
1 medium tomato, peeled, seeded & chopped
5 eggs
1 t. seasoned salt
½ t. garlic powder
½ t. prepared mustard
½ t. cayenne pepper
1½ c. milk

Butter a 13"x9" baking dish. Layer 7 slices of bread on bottom of dish. Sprinkle half of cheddar cheese over bread slices. Next, layer thawed chopped broccoli, onion, ham & tomato over cheese & bread layers. Top with remaining cheese & bread slices. In mixing bowl, combine remaining ingredients; beat well. Pour egg mixture over layered ingredients in baking dish. Cover & refrigerate at least 3 hours or overnight. Bake in 350° oven for 40-50 minutes or until knife inserted in center comes out clean.

Mmmm! ~ Serves 8-10 people (and one dog)

Why use everybody-has-'em, regular old cake pans and casserole dishes? Don't settle for boring...find something beautiful in stoneware or granite to cook in!

CHICKEN STEW

Let the cooker do all the work for you!

2 sweet potatoes, peeled and
   chopped
1 onion, sliced
6 boneless chicken breasts
$1/2$ t. dried thyme
$1/4$ t. pepper
2 bay leaves
$3^{1}/_2$ c. water, divided
2 3-oz. pkgs. chicken ramen
   noodles with seasoning
   packets

In a 3-quart slow cooker, layer
potatoes, onion and chicken.
Sprinkle with thyme and pepper.
Add bay leaves. Combine one cup
water and seasoning packets from
noodle soup, reserving noodles.
Pour seasoning over chicken; add
remaining water to stockpot. Cover
and cook on low heat 7 hours. Stir
in reserved noodles; turn heat to
high and cook 10 minutes. Remove
bay leaves before serving.

Joanne West
Beavercreek, OH

I'm in SUCH a Stew!

Reuben Casserole

REUBEN CASSEROLE

*A favorite sandwich turned into
a casserole!*

2 $14^{1}/_2$-oz. cans sauerkraut,
   drained
2 12-oz. cans corned beef,
   crumbled
4 c. Swiss cheese, shredded
   and divided
1 c. mayonnaise
1 c. Thousand Island dressing
4 T. butter, melted
$1/2$ c. soft rye bread crumbs
$1/2$ t. caraway seeds

Layer sauerkraut, corned beef and
half the cheese in a 13"x9" baking
dish. Mix mayonnaise and dressing
together; pour over casserole
mixture. Sprinkle with remaining
cheese. Mix together butter and
bread crumbs; sprinkle over top.
Sprinkle with caraway seeds. Bake
at 375 degrees for 30 minutes.

Phyllis Laughrey
Mount Vernon, OH

SOUR CREAM TACOS

A wonderful way to use leftover turkey.

1 onion, chopped
2 T. oil
1 to 2 c. chicken broth
4 to 6 canned jalapeño peppers,
　　chopped
1 t. salt
1/2 t. pepper
3 c. cooked turkey or chicken,
　　diced
2 c. sour cream
1 lb. American cheese, shredded
2 14 1/2-oz. cans tomatoes,
　　chopped
12 corn tortillas, torn
1 c. Cheddar cheese, shredded

Sauté onion in oil; add chicken
broth, jalapeño peppers, salt and
pepper. Mix turkey, sour cream,
American cheese and tomatoes
together. Add onion mixture
to turkey mixture, along with
the torn tortillas; mix well.
Place in a 13"x9" baking pan.
Bake at 350 degrees for
30 to 40 minutes. The last
10 minutes of baking, top with
the Cheddar cheese. Serves 6.

Neta Liebscher
El Reno, OK

*"One makes one's own
happiness only by taking care
of the happiness of others."*
— Saint-Pierre

SPAGHETTI CASSEROLE

*Feeds a crowd and can be made ahead
and refrigerated before baking.*

1 c. onion, chopped
1 c. green pepper, chopped
1 T. butter
28-oz. can tomatoes, undrained
4-oz. can mushrooms, drained
3.8-oz. can sliced, black olives,
　　drained
2 t. dried oregano
1 lb. ground beef, browned and
　　drained
12 oz. spaghetti, cooked and
　　drained
2 c. Cheddar cheese, shredded
10 3/4-oz. can condensed cream of
　　mushroom soup
1/4 c. water
1/4 c. grated Parmesan cheese

In a large skillet, sauté onion and
green pepper in butter until tender.
Add tomatoes, mushrooms, olives
and oregano. Add ground beef and
simmer, uncovered, for 10 minutes.
Place half of the spaghetti in a
greased 13"x9" baking dish. Top
with half of the vegetable mixture.
Sprinkle with one cup of Cheddar
cheese. Repeat layers. Combine
soup and water; stir until smooth.
Pour over casserole. Sprinkle with
Parmesan cheese. Bake, uncovered,
at 350 degrees for 30 to
55 minutes or until heated
through. Makes 12 servings.

Laura Strausberger
Cary, IL

Spotty's SPEEDY SPANISH SKILLET

...a one-pan wonder!

1 small green pepper, cut in strips
1 T. butter
2 15-oz. cans Spanish rice
12-oz. can whole kernel corn, drained
1 1/2 t. minced dried onion
3/4 c. canned black beans, rinsed
16-oz. can Mexican-style
　　tomatoes, chopped

1/2 t. Worcestershire sauce
dash ground red pepper
few dashes of hot sauce
3/4 c. sharp Cheddar cheese,
　　grated

★

Cook green pepper in butter
until tender. Stir in remaining
ingredients except cheese. Heat
through. Sprinkle cheese on top
just before serving.

¡olé!

HOLIDAY ETIQUETTE:
Please Remove Antlers before being seated at Christmas dinner.

*Clean up as you go. Table
salt poured on an oven spill
will make it easier to clean up
later. A damp sponge makes
a great spoon rest.*

INSTRUCTIONS

PHOTO ORNAMENTS
(shown on pages 8 and 9)

- old photographs
- photo transfer paper
- white fabric
- print homespun fabric
- fusible interfacing
- scraps of muslin
- permanent fine-point markers
- decorative-edge craft scissors
- medium-weight cardboard
- low-loft polyester batting
- hot glue gun
- fabric-covered welting
- black felt
- fabric glue
- ³/₄-inch wide grosgrain ribbon
- charms
- greenery sprigs

Use fabric glue for all gluing unless otherwise indicated.

1. Have a copy shop transfer your photos onto photo transfer paper.

2. Follow manufacturer's instructions to transfer photos onto white fabric...fuse interfacing to wrong side of transferred photos and to the back of muslin pieces for nameplates.

3. Use markers to write names or dates on nameplates; draw "stitched" borders around names, then draw wavy borders around photos. Use craft scissors to cut out photos and nameplates just outside borders.

4. For each ornament, cut a piece from cardboard to accommodate photo and nameplate. Cut a piece from batting the same size as cardboard piece and a piece from homespun one inch larger on all sides than cardboard piece. Place fabric wrong side up on a flat surface. Center batting, then cardboard on fabric; fold fabric edges to the back of cardboard and hot glue to secure. Beginning and ending at top center, hot glue flange of welting to back side of ornament along edges.

5. Arrange and glue photos and nameplates on ornaments. Cut triangles from felt for picture corners; glue corners to photos and allow to dry.

6. For hanger, hot glue ends of a 6-inch length of ribbon to back of ornament. Hot glue charms, a ribbon bow and greenery to ornament as desired.

7. Cut a piece from fabric ¹/₂ inch smaller than ornament. Glue fabric over back of ornament.

PHOTO PILLOW ORNAMENT
(shown on page 10)

- photograph
- photo transfer paper
- scrap of muslin
- fusible interfacing
- red and green print fabrics
- red and green embroidery floss
- polyester fiberfill
- one yard of ³/₄-inch wide grosgrain ribbon

Use a ¹/₂-inch seam allowance for all sewing unless otherwise indicated. Refer to Embroidery Stitches, page 133, before beginning project.

1. Have a copy shop transfer your photo onto photo transfer paper.

2. Following manufacturer's instructions and aligning edges with grain of muslin, transfer photo onto muslin. Cut a piece of interfacing ¹/₄ inch larger than photo. Center and fuse interfacing to back of transferred photo. Cut out photo ¹/₄ inch outside edge of interfacing; pull threads to fringe edges.

3. For pillow top, cut four 5-inch squares from print fabrics. Matching wrong sides, sew squares together to form a 9-inch square pillow top.

4. Pin photo at center of pillow top. Using 3 strands of floss, work one red *French Knot* berry and 2 green *Lazy Daisy* leaves at each corner of photo. Trim pillow top 2¹/₂ inches outside edges of photo. For backing, cut a piece of fabric the same size as pillow top.

5. Matching wrong sides and leaving an opening for turning, sew pillow top and back together...clip corners and turn right side out. Stuff pillow with fiberfill; tack opening closed.

6. Tie a bow at center of ribbon. Sew knot of bow to back of pillow at top and sew streamers to back of pillow at bottom.

SHUTTER CARD DISPLAY
(shown on page 13)

- spray primer
- red spray paint
- set of wooden shutters
- white acrylic paint
- old toothbrush
- homespun fabrics
- craft glue
- assorted buttons

Allow primer, paint and glue to dry after each application.

1. Apply primer, then red spray paint to shutters. *Spatter Paint*, page 134, shutters with white paint.

2. Tear strips of homespun to fit edges and center supports of shutters; glue strips in place. Glue buttons along strips as desired.

3. Arrange card holder with slates opening upward; place cards on holder.

PHOTO TRAY
(shown on page 14)

- wooden frame with glass and back (we used a 15"x18" frame)
- drill and bits
- 2 drawer pulls
- black spray paint
- paste floor wax
- ivory acrylic paint
- paintbrushes
- fine-grit sandpaper
- tack cloth
- wood-tone spray
- clear acrylic spray sealer
- assorted fabrics
- paper-backed fusible web
- spray adhesive
- photograph 4 inches smaller than opening of frame
- staple gun
- craft glue
- assorted buttons

Allow paint, wood-tone spray, sealer and glue to dry after each application.

1. Remove glass and back from frame. Drill holes on short sides of frame, spaced to fit pulls.

2. Spray paint frame black. Apply a thin layer of wax over frame, then paint frame ivory. Lightly sand frame for a slightly aged look, then wipe with tack cloth. Apply wood-tone spray, then 2 to 3 coats of sealer to frame.

3. Attach pulls to frame.

4. Cut pieces from fabric and web the same size as backing from frame...fuse web to wrong side of fabric. Cut another piece of fabric one-inch smaller on all sides than backing and a piece of web $1^1/_4$ inch smaller on all sides than backing. Center and fuse the web to the wrong side of the fabric...pull threads to fringe edges. Centering smaller fabric piece on top, fuse fabric pieces to backing.

5. Apply spray adhesive to back of photo. Center and smooth photo on backing. Place glass and backing in frame, then staple along edges on back of frame to secure backing. Glue buttons to frame as desired.

MEMORY ALBUM
(shown on page 15)

Capture treasured memories in a handcrafted photo album. Start with pages of card stock for the photo pages; glue on photos backed with festive papers. Then, use a pencil to draw fun pictures and write memories from the day...don't forget to add the date. Use a permanent marker to go over your work.

For the cover, embellish embossed card stock with corrugated craft cardboard cut-outs and card stock banners. Stack the pages and covers together and punch holes for the binding. For each hole, place a button on each side of the hole and use floss to sew through the holes of the buttons; knot the floss ends on the back to secure.

TICKING CANDY CANES
(shown on pages 16 and 17)

- tracing paper
- red & white ticking
- assorted white buttons
- pinking shears
- polyester fiberfill

1. Trace candy cane pattern, page 136, onto tracing paper. Matching wrong sides, fold one edge of ticking over 10 inches. For each candy cane, pin pattern to folded area of fabric so stripes on fabric run diagonally across pattern; cut out $1/2$ inch outside pattern.

2. Sew buttons down center of one candy cane shape if desired.

3. Using a $1/2$-inch seam allowance and leaving an opening for stuffing, sew pieces together. Use pinking shears to trim seam to $1/8$ inch. Firmly stuff candy cane with fiberfill, then sew opening closed.

POPCORN GARLAND
(shown on pages 16 and 17)

Quick & easy...that's what this old-fashioned tree trimming is. Use a needle to string popped corn (stale popcorn doesn't break as easily) and artificial cranberries on heavy thread.

FELT REDBIRDS
(shown on pages 16 and 17)

- tracing paper
- red felt
- fabric for wings
- gold embroidery floss
- assorted buttons
- polyester fiberfill
- hot glue gun
- $3/4$-inch long twigs for feet
- 4-inch long twigs for legs
- white acrylic paint
- stiff paintbrush

1. Trace bird and wing patterns, page 136, onto tracing paper.

2. For each bird, use patterns to cut 2 bodies from felt and one wing from fabric.

3. On one body piece, use floss to sew on a button for an eye and sew through a button to secure wing to body. Aligning body pieces and leaving an opening for stuffing, use 3 strands of floss to work Blanket Stitches, page 133, along edges of bird; lightly stuff with fiberfill and sew opening closed.

4. Glue feet to bottom of legs. Follow Dry Brush, page 134, to paint legs white; allow to dry. Glue tops of legs between body pieces on bottom of bird.

SNOWFLAKE DOOR BASKET
(shown on page 19)

- 4-inch dia. paper doilies
- small sharp scissors
- craft glue
- hot glue gun
- close-up photographs
- brown paper-covered wire
- medium-weight cardboard
- fabric
- white card stock
- red corrugated craft cardboard
- decorative-edge craft scissors
- button
- permanent fine-point marker
- grapevine door basket
- fresh greenery

Use craft glue for all gluing unless otherwise indicated.

1. For each snowflake, use at least 3 plies of doily (several plies usually stick together). Use scissors to carefully cut away doily sections as desired to create snowflakes (our snowflakes are all made from identical doilies).

2. Trim photo and glue to center of snowflake. Hot glue one end of wire to back of snowflake.

3. For sign, cover a $4^1/2$"x$5^1/2$" piece of cardboard with a 5"x6" piece of fabric; glue edges to back of cardboard. Center and glue a $2^1/2$"x$3^1/4$" piece of card stock onto craft cardboard; use craft scissors to trim cardboard to $1/4$ inch outside edges of card stock. Glue craft cardboard to center of fabric-covered cardboard. Tie an 8-inch long fabric strip into a bow; glue bow to tag and a button to knot of bow. Use marker to write message on the tag.

4. Arrange greenery, snowflakes and sign in basket as desired.

FRAMED AND WINDOW SNOWFLAKES

(shown on pages 20 and 21)

- white paper for snowflakes
- tracing paper
- transfer paper
- craft knife or small sharp scissors
- spray adhesive
- iridescent micro-glitter
- mat board
- wooden picture frames
- red and green plaid fabrics
- craft glue
- white buttons
- clear nylon thread

1. Begin with a 6¹⁄₂-inch square of white paper for each framed snowflake and a 9¹⁄₂-inch square of paper for each window snowflake; refer to Figs. 1 through 5 to fold your paper into a triangle shape.

Fig. 1

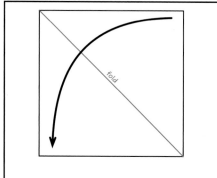

Fig. 2

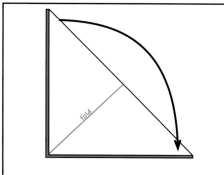

Fig. 3

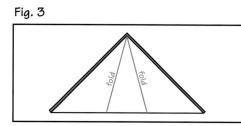

Fig. 4

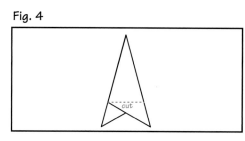

Fig. 5

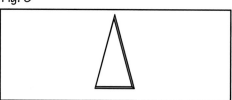

2. Trace desired snowflake pattern, page 148, onto tracing paper (if making framed snowflakes, enlarge the patterns 50% on a photo copier, then trace onto tracing paper). Aligning solid red line on pattern with folded edge of triangle, use transfer paper to transfer design to triangle; use craft knife or scissors to cut away black areas of pattern. Gently unfold snowflake and press.

3. Apply spray adhesive to one side of snowflake, then cover snowflake with glitter. Gently shake snowflake to remove excess glitter.

4. To mount snowflake for framing, cut a piece from mat board to fit in frame. Cut a piece of fabric the same size as mat board. Apply spray adhesive to wrong side of fabric...smooth fabric onto mat board. Apply spray adhesive to wrong side of snowflake; carefully center and smooth snowflake onto fabric side of mat board. Glue buttons to snowflake. Secure snowflake in frame.

5. To mount snowflakes in window, use thread to make desired length hanger for each snowflake.

EMBROIDERED MUSLIN STOCKING

(shown on page 34)

- tracing paper
- muslin
- cream, green and brown pearl cotton
- assorted buttons

Refer to Embroidery Stitches, page 133, before beginning project.

1. Trace stocking, star and tree patterns, page 139, onto tracing paper. Pin the pattern to 3 layers of muslin; cut out 3 stocking shapes.

2. Remove pattern and baste 2 stocking pieces together for stocking front. Pin pattern to stocking front. Referring to floss color on pattern and using pearl cotton, work *French Knots* over dots and *Straight Stitches* for snowflakes, then *Couch* pearl cotton along tree, star and stocking cuff. *Couch* pearl cotton over center of each large snowflake. Carefully tear away pattern.

3. Sew buttons along top of stocking and down tree.

4. Matching right sides and leaving top open, sew stocking front and back pieces together; clip curves and turn stocking right side out.

5. Press top of stocking ¹⁄₄ inch to the wrong side; *Blind Stitch* in place.

6. For hanger, braid two 6-inch lengths of each color pearl cotton together; knot and fray ends. Tack ends of hanger to heel seam of stocking.

KNIT STOCKINGS

(shown on page 35)

Abbreviations

K	knit
mm	millimeters
P	purl
PSSO	pass slipped stitch over
st(s)	stitches
tog	together

( ) – worked enclosed instructions **as many times** as specified by the number immediately following **or** work all enclosed instructions in the stitch or space indicated **or** contains explanatory remarks.

SANTA STOCKING

Materials

- Worsted Weight Yarn:
  Beige Heather - 3 ounces, (90 grams, 190 yards)
  Red - 1¼ ounces, (40 grams, 95 yards)
  Winter White - 15 yards
  Green - 10 yards
  Blue - 5 yards
  Black - 5 yards
  Gold, Peach & Brown - small amount of **each**
- straight knitting needles, size 7 (4.50 mm) or size needed for gauge
- bobbins
- 3 stitch holders
- markers
- yarn needle

Gauge: In Stockinette Stitch, 20 sts and 26 rows = 4 inches

Top

With Red, cast on 68 sts **loosely**.

Rows 1-6: Beginning with a **knit** row, work in Stockinette Stitch (knit one row, purl one row).

Row 7 (Eyelet row): K1, (YO, K2 tog) across to last st, K1.

Rows 8-14: Work in Stockinette Stitch for 7 rows.

Leg

Rows 15-88: Starting with a **knit** row and working even in Stockinette Stitch, follow Santa chart, page 140.
Cut yarn.

Left Heel

*When instructed to slip a stitch, always slip as if to **purl** unless otherwise specified.*

Row 1: Slip 16 sts onto st holder (Right Heel), slip 36 sts onto second st holder (top of Foot), slip 1, with Red, knit across: 16 sts.

Row 2: Purl across.

Row 3: Slip 1, knit across.

Rows 4-15: Repeat Rows 2 and 3, 6 times.

Short Rows (form corner of Heel): P2, P2 tog, P1, turn; slip 1, K3, turn; P3, P2 tog, P1, turn; slip 1, K4, turn; P4, P2 tog, P1, turn; slip 1, K5, turn; P5, P2 tog, P1, turn; slip 1, K6, turn; P6, P2 tog, P1, turn; slip 1, K7, turn; P7, P2 tog, P1, turn; slip 1, K8, turn; P8, P2 tog; cut yarn: 9 sts.

Slip remaining sts onto st holder.

Right Heel

With **right** side facing, slip sts from Right Heel st holder onto empty needle.

Row 1: With Red, knit across.

Row 2: Slip 1, purl across.

Rows 3-14: Repeat Rows 1 and 2, 6 times.

Short Rows: K2, slip 1 as if to **knit**, K1, PSSO, K1, turn; slip 1, P3, turn; K3, slip 1 as if to **knit**, K1, PSSO, K1, turn; slip 1, P4, turn; K4, slip 1 as if to **knit**, K1, PSSO, K1, turn; slip 1, P5, turn; K5, slip 1 as if to **knit**, K1, PSSO, K1, turn; slip 1, P6, turn; K6, slip 1 as if to **knit**, K1, PSSO, K1, turn; slip 1, P7, turn; K7, slip 1 as if to **knit**, K1, PSSO, K1, turn; slip 1, P8, turn; K8, slip 1 as if to **knit**, K1, PSSO; cut yarn: 9 sts.

Gusset and Instep Shaping

Row 1: With Beige Heather, pick up 7 sts on inside of Right Heel, slip 36 sts from next st holder (top of Foot) onto empty needle and knit across, pick up 7 sts on inside edge of Left Heel, slip 9 sts from Left Heel st holder onto empty needle and knit across: 68 sts.

Row 2 AND ALL WRONG SIDE ROWS: Purl across.

Row 3: K 15, K2 tog, K 34, slip 1 as if to **knit**, K1, PSSO, K 15: 66 sts.

Row 5: K 14, K2 tog, K 34, slip 1 as if to **knit**, K1, PSSO, K 14: 64 sts.

Row 7: K 13, K2 tog, K 34, slip 1 as if to **knit**, K1, PSSO, K 13: 62 sts.

Row 9: K 12, K2 tog, K 34, slip 1 as if to **knit**, K1, PSSO, K 12: 60 sts.

Row 11: K 11, K2 tog, K 34, slip 1 as if to **knit**, K1, PSSO, K 11: 58 sts.

Row 13: K 10, K2 tog, K 34, slip 1 as if to **knit**, K1, PSSO, K 10: 56 sts.

Rows 14-40: Work in Stockinette Stitch for 27 rows.
Cut yarn.

Toe Shaping

Row 1: With Red K 11, K2 tog, K1, place marker, K1, slip 1 as if to **knit**, K1, PSSO, K 22, K2 tog, K1, place marker, K1, slip 1 as if to **knit**, K1, PSSO, K 11: 52 sts.

Row 2: Purl across.

Row 3: (Knit across to within 3 sts of marker, K2 tog, K2, slip 1 as if to **knit**, K1, PSSO) twice, knit across: 48 sts.

Row 4: Purl across.

Rows 5-18: Repeat Rows 3 and 4, 7 times: 20 sts.

Bind off remaining sts.

Finishing

With Blue, add French Knots for eyes.

With a double strand of Winter White, add French Knot pom-pom to hat.

With **right** sides together, sew seam.

For stocking top, fold top edge to **wrong** side along Eyelet Row and sew in place.

For hanging loop, braid three 6-inch lengths of Red yarn and attach to seam.

SNOWMAN STOCKING

Materials

- Worsted Weight Yarn:
  Beige Heather - 2¼ ounces, (70 grams, 140 yards)
  Red - ¾ ounces, (20 grams, 45 yards)
  Blue - ¾ ounces, (20 grams, 45 yards)
  Green - 10 yards
  Winter White - 15 yards
  Gold, Black & Brown - small amount of **each**
- straight knitting needles, size 7 (4.50 mm) or size needed for gauge
- bobbins
- 3 stitch holders
- markers
- yarn needle

Gauge: In Stockinette Stitch, 20 sts and 26 rows = 4 inches

Top

With Red, cast on 68 sts **loosely**.

Rows 1-6: Beginning with a **knit** row, work in Stockinette Stitch (knit one row, purl one row).

Row 7 (Eyelet row): K1, (YO, K2 tog) across to last st, K1.

Rows 8-14: Work in Stockinette Stitch for 7 rows.

Leg

Rows 15-84: Starting with a **knit** row and working even in Stockinette Stitch, follow Snowman chart, page 141.
Cut yarn.

(continued on page 124)

Left Heel

*When instructed to slip a stitch, always slip as if to **purl** unless otherwise specified.*

Row 1: Slip 16 sts onto st holder (Right Heel), slip 36 sts onto second st holder (top of Foot), slip 1, with Blue, knit across: 16 sts.

Row 2: Purl across.

Row 3: Slip 1, knit across.

Rows 4-15: Repeat Rows 2 and 3, 6 times.

Short Rows (form corner of Heel): P2, P2 tog, P1, turn; slip 1, K3, turn; P3, P2 tog, P1, turn; slip 1, K4, turn; P4, P2 tog, P1, turn; slip 1, K5, turn; P5, P2 tog, P1, turn; slip 1, K6, turn; P6, P2 tog, P1, turn; slip 1, K7, turn; P7, P2 tog, P1, turn; slip 1, K8, turn; P8, P2 tog; cut yarn: 9 sts.

Slip remaining sts onto st holder.

Right Heel

With **right** side facing, slip sts from Right Heel st holder onto empty needle.

Row 1: With Blue, knit across.

Row 2: Slip 1, purl across.

Rows 3-14: Repeat Rows 1 and 2, 6 times.

Short Rows: K2, slip 1 as if to **knit**, K1, PSSO, K1, turn; slip 1, P3, turn; K3, slip 1 as if to **knit**, K1, PSSO, K1, turn; slip 1, P4, turn; K4, slip 1 as if to **knit**, K1, PSSO, K1, turn; slip 1, P5, turn; K5, slip 1 as if to **knit**, K1, PSSO, K1, turn; slip 1, P6, turn; K6, slip 1 as if to **knit**, K1, PSSO, K1, turn; slip 1, P7, turn; K7, slip 1 as if to **knit**, K1, PSSO, K1, turn; slip 1, P8, turn; K8, slip 1 as if to **knit**, K1, PSSO; cut yarn: 9 sts.

Gusset and Instep Shaping

Row 1: With Beige Heather, pick up 7 sts on inside of Right Heel, slip 36 sts from next st holder (top of Foot) onto empty needle and knit across, pick up 7 sts on inside edge of Left Heel, knit 9 sts from Left Heel st holder onto empty needle and knit across: 68 sts.

Row 2 AND ALL WRONG SIDE ROWS: Purl across.

Row 3: K 15, K2 tog, K 34, slip 1 as if to **knit**, K1, PSSO, K 15: 66 sts.

Row 5: K 14, K2 tog, K 34, slip 1 as if to **knit**, K1, PSSO, K 14: 64 sts.

Row 7: K 13, K2 tog, K 34, slip 1 as if to **knit**, K1, PSSO, K 13: 62 sts.

Row 9: K 12, K2 tog, K 34, slip 1 as if to **knit**, K1, PSSO, K 12: 60 sts.

Row 11: K 11, K2 tog, K 34, slip 1 as if to **knit**, K1, PSSO, K 11: 58 sts.

Row 13: K 10, K2 tog, K 34, slip 1 as if to **knit**, K1, PSSO, K 10: 56 sts.

Rows 14-40: Work in Stockinette Stitch for 27 rows.
Cut yarn.

Toe Shaping

Row 1: With Blue K 11, K2 tog, K1, place marker, K1, slip 1 as if to **knit**, K1, PSSO, K 22, K2 tog, K1, place marker, K1, slip 1 as if to **knit**, K1, PSSO, K 11: 52 sts.

Row 2: Purl across.

Row 3: (Knit across to within 3 sts of marker, K2 tog, K2, slip 1 as if to **knit**, K1, PSSO) twice, knit across: 48 sts.

Row 4: Purl across.

Rows 5-18: Repeat Rows 3 and 4, 7 times: 20 sts.

Bind off remaining sts.

Finishing

With Black, add French Knots for eyes, nose, and buttons.

With **right** sides together, sew seam.

For stocking top, fold top edge to **wrong** side along Eyelet Row and sew in place.

For hanging loop, braid three 6-inch lengths of Red yarn and attach to seam.

BUTTON WREATH

(shown on pages 36 and 37)

- white spray paint
- 18-inch dia. plastic, flat-backed wreath
- hot glue gun
- lots of assorted white buttons
- iridescent glitter paint
- paintbrush
- pinking shears
- gingham fabric
- embroidery floss to match fabric

1. Glue lots and lots of white buttons to wreath, overlapping as necessary for desired coverage.

2. Paint buttons and wreath with glitter paint as desired; set aside to dry.

3. For bow loop, use pinking shears to cut a 4"x22" strip from fabric. Matching wrong sides and overlapping ends one inch, fold ends of strip to the center. Tie floss tightly around overlapped area. For knot, cut a 2¼"x5" strip from fabric; press long edges ¼ inch to wrong side. Overlapping ends at back, glue strip over gathers of loops. For streamers, cut a 2½"x17½" strip from fabric: glue center of strip to back of bow. Glue bow to the wreath…notch streamer ends.

TICKING TREE

(continued from page 41)

Star Ornaments

- tracing paper
- tan ticking
- round and heart-shaped buttons
- embroidery floss
- rattail cord
- polyester fiberfill
- pinking shears

Refer to Embroidery Stitches, page 133, before beginning project. Use 3 strands of floss for all stitching.

1. Trace small star pattern, page 142, onto tracing paper. For each star, use pattern to cut 2 stars from ticking.

2. If desired, lightly pencil a favorite word of the season on the right side of one star shape, Work *Backstitches* over the word, or add a bow-tied button or heart button at the center of the star.

3. For the hanger, knot the ends of a 7-inch length of cord together. Matching wrong sides of star, pin knot of hanger between star front and back at top point. Leaving an opening for stuffing, work *Running Stitches* along the edges of the star to sew pieces together.

4. Lightly stuff star with fiberfill, then sew opening closed. Use pinking shears to trim edges of stars.

Tree Skirt

- 28-inch square of gingham fabric
- string
- chalk pencil
- thumbtack
- pinking shears
- lace
- tissue paper
- embroidery floss

1. Matching right sides, fold fabric in half from top to bottom and again from left to right.

2. Tie one end of string to chalk pencil. Insert thumbtack through string 15 inches from the pencil. Insert thumbtack through the fabric as shown in Fig. 1; mark the outside cutting line.

Fig. 1

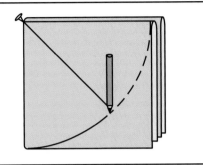

3. Repeat Step 2, inserting thumbtack 2 inches from pencil; mark inner cutting line. Use pinking shears to cut along drawn lines through all layers of fabric.

4. Draw a straight line from inner circle to outer edge...use pinking shears to cut skirt open along line.

5. Sew lace along outer edges of circle.

6. Trace words, page 143, onto tissue paper desired of number times. Arrange and pin patterns along outer edge of skirt. Use 3 strands of floss to work *Backstitches* over words. Carefully tear away patterns.

TICKING STOCKING
(shown on page 42)

- tracing paper
- 15"x22" pieces of tan ticking and lining fabric
- vintage crocheted lace
- jute
- embroidery floss
- assorted buttons

Use a ¹/₄-inch seam allowance for all sewing unless otherwise indicated.

1. Following *Making Patterns*, page 134, and using the stocking pattern on page 146, draw a complete stocking pattern on tracing paper. Cut out pattern ¹/₄ inch outside drawn lines. Matching right sides and long edges, fold ticking

and lining in half; stack fabrics together. Pin pattern to fabrics; cut out stocking and lining pieces.

2. Sew stocking pieces together; clip curves and turn right side out. Repeat to sew lining pieces together; do not turn. Press top edge of stocking and lining ¹/₄ inch to wrong side. Matching seams and top edges, place lining in stocking. *Blind Stitch*, page 133, top edges together to secure.

3. For cuff, cut a 16-inch piece from lace; match short edges and sew together. Matching cuff seam with heel seam on stocking, pin cuff to stocking. *Blind Stitch* cuff to top edge of stocking.

4. For hanger, knot ends of an 8-inch length of jute together. Sew knot of hanger to inside of stocking at heel seam.

5. Use 3 strands of floss to sew buttons to cuff as desired.

CHICKEN FEEDER CANDLEHOLDER
(shown on page 51)

- trough-style chicken feeder
- household cement
- craft steel
- tracing paper
- utility scissors
- white spray primer
- white spray paint
- wood-tone spray
- clear acrylic spray sealer
- homespun fabric
- hot glue gun
- fresh greenery
- fresh red pears
- fresh red and green apples
- taper candles
- birdseed

Allow cement, paint, wood-tone spray and sealer to dry after each application.

1. Using household cement to piece strips as necessary, cut 2 one inch wide strips of craft steel to fit long edges of feeder. Trace the scallop pattern, page 139, onto tracing paper; cut out. Beginning at the center and working outward, use pattern to mark scallops along top edge of steel strips. Use utility scissors to cut along scallops. Use household cement to glue strips along inside edges of feeder.

2. Spray feeder with primer, then white paint. Lightly spray feeder with wood-tone spray, then 2 to 3 coats of sealer.

3. Piecing as necessary, tear a strip of homespun to go around feeder...glue strip around feeder.

4. Tie a strip torn from homespun into a bow. Glue bow to center front of feeder. Glue greenery to knot of bow.

5. Hollow out some of the fruit for candleholders and insert tapers. Fill the feeder with birdseed; arrange fruits and candleholders in the feeder.

CUT-OUT TAGS AND CARDS
(shown on pages 54 and 55)

Tags
- smooth and embossed card stock
- decorative-edge craft scissors
- assorted buttons
- permanent fine-point markers
- craft glue
- craft knife and cutting mat
- fabric scraps
- tracing paper
- brown kraft paper
- rickrack

Use straight-edge or decorative-edge scissors, as desired, to cut out tags.

1. Photocopy tag designs, page 135, onto card stock; cut out tags.

2. For heart tag, sew buttons to tag, then write name on tag. Glue tag to embossed card stock. Trim card stock to ¹/₄ inch outside edge of tag.

3. For sewn star tags, use craft knife to cut out large star from tag. Glue fabric over star on back side of tag; sew a button at center of star. Place tag on card stock and sew along edges. Trim background card stock close to tag.

4. For sewn heart tag, trace the heart from tag onto tracing paper; cut out. Using pattern, cut heart from red card stock; glue heart to tag. Place tag on card stock and sew along edges. Trim background card stock close to tag.

(continued on page 126)

5. For block name tag, write name on small squares of kraft paper; trim squares to fit on tag. Glue name to tag, then embellish with rickrack and sewn-on buttons. Glue tag to card stock, then draw a "stitched" border. Trim background card stock close to border.

6. For hanging tag, write name on a strip of kraft paper. Draw sprinkles of stars and dots around name; cut out. Glue strip to a piece of card stock. Draw a "stitched" border around strip; cut out. Catching the ends of a piece of rickrack, sew a button at top of tag. Glue tag to another piece of card stock and cut out.

Cards

- 8¹/₂"x 11" card stock with envelopes to fit bi-fold cards
- craft knife and cutting mat
- fabric scraps
- craft glue

1. Photocopy card designs, page 147, onto card stock. Cut out card fronts along outer lines. Use a craft knife to carefully cut shapes from card fronts.

2. Cut pieces from fabric scraps large enough to cover cut out shapes; glue over cut-outs on back of card front.

3. Fold another piece of card stock in half; unfold. Center and sew card front on front of card stock.

COPPER-TOP GIFT BOXES
(shown on page 57)

- desired colors of acrylic paint
- paintbrushes
- paper maché box with lid to fit desired design from page 137 or 148
- clear acrylic spray sealer
- tracing paper
- removable tape
- craft-weight copper sheet
- corrugated cardboard
- stylus
- stencil brush
- black stencil cream
- soft cloth
- decorative-edge craft scissors
- craft glue

Allow paint, sealer and glue to dry after each application.

1. Paint box and lid as desired. Apply sealer to box and lid.

2. Trace truck or snowman pattern, pages 137 or 148, onto tracing paper. Tape pattern to copper, then tape copper to cardboard. Use stylus to draw over pattern lines; remove pattern.

3. Use stencil brush to apply stencil cream over design…leaving cream in lines, wipe off excess cream with a soft cloth.

4. Remove copper from cardboard. Use craft scissors to trim edges of copper piece. Center and glue copper piece on lid.

KITCHEN ANGEL
(shown on page 58)

- craft saw
- 13-inch wooden spoon
- ¹/₂-liter plastic bottle
- flesh-tone acrylic paint
- paintbrushes
- tracing paper
- transfer paper
- red and black permanent fine-point markers
- hot glue gun
- curly doll hair
- sand
- fabric
- embroidery floss to coordinate with fabric
- utility scissors
- 2 small metal measuring spoons
- craft wire
- lace scraps
- star-shaped button
- brown card stock
- 3-inch dia. grapevine wreath
- small basket with handle
- miniature kitchen utensils

1. For head, use a saw to trim handle of wooden spoon so spoon rests on bottle opening when handle is placed in bottle. Paint spoon flesh color and allow to dry.

2. Trace face pattern, page 149, onto tracing paper; use transfer paper to transfer face to back of spoon. Use red marker to draw over lips and black marker to draw over remaining lines…lightly color cheeks red.

3. Arrange and glue hair on head.

4. Fill bottle with sand. Insert handle of spoon in bottle; fill opening of bottle with hot glue to hold head in place.

5. For dress, tear an 11"x12" piece from fabric. Matching wrong sides and short edges and using a ¹/₄ inch seam allowance,

sew back of dress together; turn right side out. Using floss, work *Running Stitches*, page 133, along top edge of dress. Place dress over bottle. Pull floss ends to gather dress at neck; knot and trim floss ends.

6. For sleeves, cut a 3"x12" piece from fabric. Press, then sew short edges of fabric piece ¹/₄ inch to the wrong side. Matching right sides and long edges, use a ¹/₄-inch seam allowance to sew edges together to form a tube; turn right side out. For hands, use utility scissors to trim handles of measuring spoons to 3 inches. Cut a 14-inch length of wire for arms. Wrap 2 inches of one end of wire around the handle of one measuring spoon. Thread arms through sleeves, then wrap 2 inches of end of wire around handle of remaining measuring spoon. Glue center of arms at back of neck.

7. Overlapping ends at back, glue a length of lace around neck for a collar. Tie a ³/₄"x8" strip torn from fabric into a bow; glue bow and a button to collar.

8. Photocopy wing pattern, page 149, onto card stock; cut out. Glue wings to back of angel.

9. Glue wreath to head for halo. Fill basket with utensils and place in angel's hands; glue to secure.

PRIMITIVE EMBROIDERED SWEATER
(shown on page 62)

- green, brown and gold embroidery floss
- tissue paper
- cotton knit sweater
- seven ³/₈-inch dia. ecru buttons
- seven ³/₄-inch dia. blue, green or gold star-shaped buttons
- eight ¹/₂-inch dia. red buttons

Work stitches through nearest "hole" in knit of sweater. Refer to Embroidery Stitches, page 133, before beginning project.

1. Trace pattern, page 152, onto tissue paper. Position and pin pattern on sweater.

2. Stitching through tissue paper and using 2 strands of floss, work brown *Running Stitches* for tree trunk and branches, green *Straight Stitches* for needles and gold *Cross Stitches* for tree base. Carefully remove tissue paper.

3. Use 2 strands of gold floss to sew buttons on tree as desired.

SNOW KID SWEATSHIRTS
(shown on page 63)

- paper-backed fusible web
- white fleece
- fabric for hat
- orange and black felt
- child-size sweatshirt
- clear nylon thread
- $3/4$-inch dia. black buttons for eyes
- white, orange, red and black embroidery floss
- $1/2$-inch dia. red buttons for mouth
- scraps of lace and ribbon (for snow girl only)
- $3/4$-inch dia. red button for hat or bow tie
- assorted white buttons

1. For each snow kid, use snowman pattern, page 153, and follow *Making Appliqués*, page 134, to make one head appliqué from fleece, hat appliqué from fabric and mouth and nose appliqués from felt. If making snow boy, make bow tie and hatband appliqués from fabric.

2. Arrange and fuse appliqués on sweatshirt. Using nylon thread, follow *Machine Appliqué*, page 134, to sew along edges of head, hat, hatband, and bow tie to secure. Sew black buttons to snow kid for eyes. Use 3 strands of white floss to make a *French Knot*, page 133, through one hole in each button for highlight in eye.

3. Using 3 strands of floss, work orange *Running Stitches*, page 133, along edges of nose, and black *Running Stitches* along mouth. Use 2 strands of red floss to sew $1/2$-inch dia. red buttons at ends of mouth.

4. For snow girl, sew a length of lace or fabric along bottom of hat. Tie 2 bows from ribbon. Sew one bow and a button to top of hat and one bow under chin.

5. For snow boy, sew a red button to center of bow tie.

6. Sew assorted white buttons to shirt for snowflakes.

STAR PILLOW
(shown on page 64)

- tracing paper
- 2 coordinating fabrics
- paper-backed fusible web
- fabric for pocket trim
- pinking shears
- embroidery floss
- assorted buttons
- polyester fiberfill

Use 3 strands of floss for all stitching.

1. Using patterns, page 154, and referring to the Assembly Diagram, page 154, make a whole star pattern and one pocket pattern from tracing paper. Using patterns, cut 2 stars from first fabric and one pocket from remaining fabric. Piecing as necessary, cut a 3"x61" strip from same fabric as stars.

2. Follow manufacturer's instructions to fuse web to fabric for pocket trim. Use pinking shears to cut a $3/4$"x$4^3/4$" strip. Press edges of pocket $1/4$ inch to the wrong side; top stitch top edge of pocket. Center and fuse trim $1/4$ inch below top of pocket. Use floss to sew 3 buttons across trim.

3. Trace words pattern, page 154, onto tracing paper. Pin pattern on pocket; work *Back Stitches*, page 133, over words. Carefully remove pattern.

4. Pin pocket at center on right side of one star piece (pillow front); use floss to work *Running Stitches*, page 133, along sides and bottom of pocket to secure.

5. Matching right sides and using a $1/2$-inch seam allowance, baste ends of strip together. Matching right sides and raw edges, pin strip along edges of pillow front. Using a $1/2$-inch seam allowance, sew strip to pillow front. Repeat for pillow back. Remove basting threads along strip seam; turn pillow right side out.

6. Sew buttons along edges of pillow front.

7. Stuff pillow with fiberfill, then sew opening closed.

THROW PILLOWS
(continued from page 65)

3. Cut a $5^1/2$"x$7^1/2$" piece from burlap; remove threads to fray edges $1/2$ inch.

4. Using tree and trunk patterns, page 136, follow *Making Appliqués*, page 134, to make 3 tree appliqués from green felt and 3 trunk appliqués from brown felt. Arrange and fuse appliqués on burlap.

5. Pin burlap on pillow top. Using 3 strands of floss, work *Running Stitches*, page 133, along burlap edges to secure. Sew a button at each corner of burlap.

6. For welting, measure around edges of pillow top; add 4 inches. Piecing as necessary, cut a 2-inch wide bias fabric strip determined measurement. Cut a piece of cord determined measurement.

7. Press one end of fabric strip $1/2$ inch to wrong side. Beginning $1/2$ inch from pressed end, center cord on wrong side of strip. Fold strip over cord. Beginning $1/2$ inch from pressed end, use a zipper foot to baste close to cord along length of strip. Trim seam allowance to $1/2$ inch.

8. Beginning with pressed end of welting and matching raw edges, pin welting to right side of pillow top (Fig. 1). Trimming to fit, insert unfinished end of welting into folded end of welting (Fig. 2). Using a zipper foot, baste welting in place close to cord.

Fig. 1

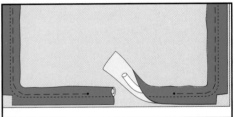

Fig. 2

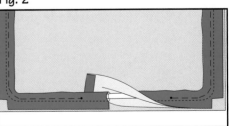

(continued on page 128)

9. Matching right sides and leaving an opening for turning, sew pillow top and pillow back together. Clip corners and turn right side out. Stuff pillow with fiberfill and sew opening closed.

Heart Pillow

1. For pillow top, cut four 10-inch squares from different fabrics. Refer to **Step 2** of **Tree Pillow** to make pillow top and pillow back.

2. Cut an 8½-inch square from burlap; remove threads to fray edges ½ inch.

3. Using heart patterns, page 136, follow *Making Appliqués*, page 134, to make one straight heart appliqué from red felt and one wavy heart appliqué from green felt. Arrange and fuse hearts on burlap. Sewing buttons to secure, cover red heart with buttons.

4. Follow **Steps 5 through 9** of **Tree Pillow** to complete pillow.

KID'S CHRISTMAS CARD KIT
(shown on page 66)

Bag
- homespun fabric
- ¼-inch wide red grosgrain ribbon
- muslin
- fusible interfacing
- paper-backed fusible web
- tracing paper
- transfer paper
- black permanent fine-point marker
- red, green and gold acrylic paint
- paintbrushes
- pinking shears
- card making supplies (we used cookie cutters, markers, tubes of glitter, decorative-edge craft scissors, craft glue sticks and crayons)

1. Cut two 8¼"x11¾" pieces from homespun. Press, then stitch all edges of each piece ¼ inch to the wrong side.

2. For casing, press top edge of each piece ¾ inch to the wrong side; stitch in place.

3. Matching right sides, using a ¼-inch seam allowance and stitching side seams below casing, sew sides and bottom of bag together. Turn bag right side out.

4. For drawstrings, cut two 22-inch lengths from ribbon. Refer to Fig. 1 to thread the drawstrings through the casings at top of bag; knot ends of each drawstring together.

Fig. 1

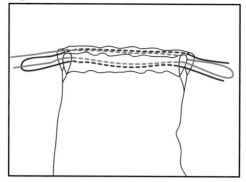

5. For bag label, cut one 3½"x6½" piece each from muslin, interfacing and web. Fuse interfacing to muslin and web to interfacing; do not remove paper backing.

6. Trace label design, page 137, onto tracing paper. Use transfer paper to transfer design to label. Use black marker to draw over transferred lines.

7. Paint design as desired; allow to dry. Use marker to go over detail lines, if necessary. Use pinking shears to trim edges of label.

8. Remove paper backing from label; fuse label to front of bag.

9. Fill bag with card-making supplies for your favorite young crafter to use for making Christmas cards.

Paper Pad
- tablet of construction paper
- pinking shears
- homespun fabric
- spray adhesive
- muslin
- fusible interfacing
- paper-backed fusible web
- tracing paper
- transfer paper
- black permanent fine-point marker
- white, flesh, red, green, gold, brown, gray and black acrylic paint
- paintbrushes

1. Measure the cover of the tablet up the front, around the spine and down the back; add 2 inches. Measure across the front of the cover; add 2 inches. Using pinking shears, cut a piece from homespun the determined measurements.

2. Apply spray adhesive to wrong side of fabric piece. With one inch of fabric extending past edges of tablet, smooth fabric onto cover. Clip fabric away at spine and cut fabric diagonally across corners; smooth edges to inside of cover.

3. For tablet label, cut one 7½"x10½" piece each from muslin, interfacing and web. Fuse interfacing to muslin and web to interfacing; do not remove paper backing.

4. Trace angel design, page 155, onto tracing paper. Use transfer paper to transfer design to label. Use a black marker to draw over transferred lines.

5. Paint design as desired; allow to dry. Use marker to go over detail lines, if necessary. Use pinking shears to trim edges of label.

6. Remove paper backing from label; fuse label to front of tablet.

DOGGIE BED
(shown on page 71)

- 3⅞ yards of 44-inch wide heavyweight fabric for cover
- string
- fabric marking pencil
- thumbtack
- dimensional fabric paint
- 1⅜ yards of 90-inch wide muslin
- 12-inch metal zipper
- cedar chips

Use a ½-inch seam allowance for all sewing unless otherwise indicated.

1. Cut a 42-inch square from cover fabric. Fold square in half from top to bottom and again from right to left. To mark cutting line for circle, tie one end of string to fabric marking pencil. Insert thumbtack through string 20½ inches from pencil. Refer to Fig. 1 to insert thumbtack in corner of fabric and mark cutting line. Cutting through all layers, cut out circle along line. Fold circle in half to use as a pattern in Step 2.

Fig. 1

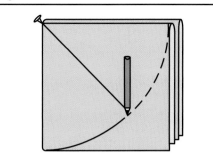

2. Cut two 27"x42" pieces from cover fabric; place fabric pieces together. Referring to Fig. 2, pin folded fabric circle on fabric pieces 5 inches from one edge and mark extended edges. Cutting through both layers, cut out half circles.

Fig. 2

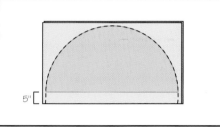

3. Press straight edge of each half circle ¼ inch to the wrong side; press 1¾ inches to wrong side again. Top stitch along pressed edges.

4. For bottom of bed, place half circles right sides up with straight edges overlapped 3 inches; pin in place. Baste overlapped edges to secure.

5. Piecing as necessary, cut two 4"x65½" strips from cover fabric. Matching right sides, sew ends of fabric strip together to form a loop. Press seam allowances to one side.

6. Matching right sides and raw edges, pin one edge of fabric strip to edge of bottom of bed. Easing in fullness, sew along curved edge. Repeat to sew top of bed to strip. Clip curves and remove basting threads along bottom; turn right side out. If desired, use dimensional paint to write name on side of bed; allow to dry.

7. For lining, cut two 45-inch squares from muslin. Inserting thumbtack 22 inches from pencil, repeat Step 2 to cut 2 circles from muslin squares. Place muslin circles together.

8. Use fabric marking pencil to mark a 12-inch zipper opening along edge of one muslin circle. Beginning and ending 5 inches beyond marks, baste along zipper line; press seam open. Center zipper, right side down, along seam between zipper marks on wrong side of muslin. Using a zipper foot, sew ¼ inch from zipper along sides, bottom and top. Remove all basting threads and open zipper.

9. Matching right sides and raw edges and leaving open at zipper, sew muslin circles together. Turn right side out through zipper opening.

10. Fill lining with cedar chips, close zipper and place lining in cover.

CAT TOYS
(shown on page 72)

Fish
- tracing paper
- gold and red felt
- pinking shears
- two ½-inch dia. green buttons
- gold and red embroidery floss
- polyester fiberfill
- catnip (optional)
- rickrack

All buttons and trims should be sewn securely for animal safety.

1. Trace fish body and fin patterns, page 151, onto tracing paper. Using pattern, cut 2 bodies from red felt. Using pinking shears, cut 2 fins from gold felt.

2. Sew one body shape to right side of each fin shape. For eyes, sew one button to right side of each body piece. Matching wrong sides and leaving an opening for stuffing, use 3 strands of gold floss to sew edges together.

3. Firmly stuff fish with fiberfill...add catnip while stuffing, if desired. Sew opening closed.

4. Tucking ends under, use 3 strands of red floss and *Running Stitches*, page 133, to sew rickrack down sides of body and around head.

Mouse
- tracing paper
- pinking shears
- mustard and red felt
- paper-backed fusible web
- ¼-inch dia. black shank buttons for eyes
- black baby rickrack
- ¾-inch dia. button
- red and black embroidery floss
- polyester fiberfill
- catnip (optional)
- heavy-duty black thread

All buttons and trims should be sewn securely for animal safety.

1. Trace body pattern, page 151, onto tracing paper. Using pinking shears, cut 2 bodies from mustard felt.

2. Using ear pattern, page 151, follow *Making Appliqués*, page 134, to make 2 ears from red felt; fuse ears to mustard felt. Use pinking shears to cut out ears just outside edge of ear.

3. Sew one eye and one ear to each body piece...make sure one side is reversed.

4. For tail, tie a knot 3 inches from one end of a 10-inch length of rickrack. Thread 3-inch end through one hole in the ¾-inch diameter button; knot the end to secure.

5. Matching wrong sides, securing button of tail between layers and leaving an opening for stuffing, use 3 strands of red floss to sew edges together.

6. Firmly stuff mouse with fiberfill...add catnip while stuffing, if desired. Sew opening closed. Trim tail to desired length, then tie a knot in end of tail.

7. For whiskers, make a stitch on one side of the nose using 2 strands of heavy-duty thread...knot the threads together to secure and trim the ends to desired length. Repeat for the opposite side.

Bell Ball
- tracing paper
- red felt
- green baby rickrack
- embroidery floss to coordinate with felt
- polyester fiberfill
- one inch dia. jingle bell
- catnip (optional)

(continued on page 130)

All trims should be sewn securely for animal safety.

1. Trace ball pattern, page 151, onto tracing paper. Use pattern to cut 3 shapes from red felt.

2. Placing rickrack between edges, match and pin one rounded edge of two pieces together. Use 3 strands of floss to sew edges together. Repeat to attach third piece to one edge. Leaving an opening for stuffing, repeat to sew remaining edges together. Firmly stuff ball with fiberfill and bell…add catnip while stuffing, if desired. Sew opening closed.

3. Tie a 12-inch length of ribbon into a bow; sew bow to top of ball.

BUTTON-RIMMED BASKET
(shown on pages 74 and 75)
- basket (we used an 8"x9" basket)
- 2 homespun fabrics
- low-loft polyester batting
- paper-backed fusible web
- hot glue gun
- lots of assorted buttons

1. For front panel, measure height and width of front of basket; cut 2 pieces from fabric determined measurements. Cut one piece from batting 1/2 inch smaller than the fabric pieces. Layer batting between wrong sides of fabric pieces. Sew pieces together 1/4 inch from edges; pull threads to fray edges.

2. Using tree pattern, page 143, follow *Making Appliqués*, page 134, to make enough tree appliqués from fabric to fit across panel. Fuse appliqués to panel, then glue one button at top of each tree. Glue panel to basket.

3. Glue buttons along rim of basket.

FABRIC WRAPPER
(shown on page 75)
Using jute to tie the ends, wrap a block of fudge in a pinked piece of fabric…glue sprigs of artificial greenery to the top. Add a hand-lettered tag made from ecru card stock on red embossed card stock, backed with corrugated craft cardboard.

SNACK BAG
(shown on page 75)
- tracing paper
- decorative lunch-size paper bag
- cardboard
- craft knife and cutting mat
- clear tape
- clear cellophane
- black permanent fine-point marker
- hot glue gun
- assorted buttons
- hole punch
- fabric
- ecru card stock
- craft glue stick
- red corrugated craft cardboard

1. Trace star pattern, page 143, onto tracing paper; cut out. Draw around pattern on front of bag desired number of times; place cardboard in bag under stars…use craft knife to cut out stars.

2. Tape a piece of cellophane large enough to cover stars on inside of bag. Use marker to draw "stitches" along edges of stars; hot glue buttons to bag.

3. Place gift in bag. Fold top of bag one inch to the front 2 times. Punch two holes one inch apart through center of folded portion of bag. Tear a 1"x12" strip from fabric; thread strip through holes and tie into a bow at front of bag.

4. Cut out a 1¼"x2" tag from card stock. Use marker to write name on tag. Use glue stick to glue tag on a piece of craft cardboard; cut out 1/4 inch outside edges of tag. Hot glue tag to bag.

SNOWFLAKE TIN
(shown on page 75)

Apply primer, then 2 to 3 coats of paint to outside of tin and lid; allow to dry. Use dimensional paint to paint "snowflakes" on tin as desired; paint a wavy line and a row of dots around edge of lid. Add a hand-lettered tag made from ecru card stock, backed with green corrugated craft cardboard.

CINNAMON CRUNCH BASKET
(shown on pages 74 and 75)
- basket (we used a 4"x8" red basket)
- fabric for liner
- pearl cotton
- assorted buttons
- spray adhesive
- 3½"x5" fabric scrap
- 3½"x5" piece of card stock
- decorative-edge craft scissors
- photocopy of tag design (page 157) on tan card stock
- 1/8-inch dia. hole punch

1. For basket liner, measure length of basket from top of rim, down side, across bottom and up opposite side; repeat to measure width of basket. Add 6 inches to each measurement; cut a piece from fabric the determined measurements.

2. Press edges of basket liner 1/4 inch to the wrong side…press 1/4 inch to wrong side again. Using 3 strands of pearl cotton, work *Running Stitches*, page 133, along pressed edges. Sew one button to each corner of liner. Place liner in basket.

3. Apply spray adhesive to wrong side of fabric scrap…smooth onto card stock piece. Use craft scissors to trim edges. Cut out tag design. Apply spray adhesive to wrong side of tag…smooth onto right side of fabric-covered card stock.

4. Punch 2 holes 1/2 inch apart at top center of tag. Use pearl cotton to attach tag to basket.

CRANBERRY BREAD BAG
(shown on page 77)
- fabrics for bag and trim
- paper-backed fusible web
- 1"x36" strip torn from fabric for bow
- photocopy of tag design (page 157) on ecru card stock
- tracing paper
- red paper
- craft glue stick
- corrugated craft cardboard
- black permanent fine-point marker

1. Cut a 17"x21" piece from fabric for bag and a 3"x21" strip from fabric for trim and fusible web. Matching long edges, fuse strip to wrong side of fabric for bag.

2. Matching right sides and short edges; fold fabric in half. Using a 1/4-inch seam allowance, sew side and bottom edges together to make bag…turn bag right side out.

3. Cut points in top of bag. Place gift in bag…tie fabric strip into a bow around top of bag.

4. Cut out tag. Trace heart shape from tag onto tracing paper. Using pattern, cut one heart from red paper; glue heart to tag. Glue tag to craft cardboard, then trim cardboard to 1/4 inch outside edges of tag. Use marker to write message on tag and draw "stitches" around heart. Glue tag to bag.

CAKE BOX

(shown on page 78)

Spruce up an ordinary cake box for the holidays. Unfold a cake box and apply spray adhesive to the right side…smooth the box onto the wrong side of a piece of wrapping paper. Use a craft knife to trim the paper around the box and cut through the slits. Refold the box and place your cake inside. Tie it up with a festive bow, add some greenery, then a handmade tag.

COOKIE MIX LABEL AND TAG

(shown on page 80)

- photocopy of label and instructions design (page 80) on ecru card stock
- craft glue
- white and red card stock
- decorative paper
- decorative-edge craft scissors
- 1/8-inch hole punch

Allow glue to dry after each application.

1. Cut out label, then glue to red card stock. Trim card stock to 1/8 inch outside edges of label. Glue label to decorative paper; use craft scissors to cut out 1/4 inch outside edges of red card stock. Glue label on jar.

2. For tag, glue instructions to wrong side of decorative paper. Use craft scissors to cut out just inside borders. Fold tag in half; punch a hole at top folded corner.

3. Tie several lengths of raffia into a bow around jar. Use raffia to attach tag to jar.

WINTERTIME SPICE TEA CUP

(shown on page 81)

- homespun fabric
- jute
- hot glue gun
- artificial holly with berries
- cinnamon sticks
- decorative-edge craft scissors
- photocopy of tag design (page 157) on ecru card stock
- craft glue stick
- red card stock
- black permanent fine-point marker

1. For bag, cut an 8 1/2"x15" piece from homespun. Matching right sides and short edges; fold fabric in half. Using a 1/4-inch seam allowance, sew side and bottom edges together to make bag…turn bag right side out. Pull threads to fray top edge of bag.

2. Place gift in bag and tie closed with a length of jute. Hot glue greenery and cinnamon sticks to knot of bow…save a little bit of greenery for the tag.

3. Use craft scissors to cut out tag 1/4 inch outside of edges of design. Using glue stick, center and glue tag to card stock…trim card stock to 1/4 inch outside edges of tag. Hot glue greenery to corner of tag…use marker to write message on tag.

PANCAKES FROM THE PANTRY

(shown on page 81)

For the tag, photocopy the tag design, page 156, onto card stock. Use decorative-edge craft scissors to cut out the tag, then glue it to embossed card stock. Trim the card stock to 1/8 inch outside the design…punch a hole in the top left corner and tie it to the gift.

MOCHA MIX BAG

(shown on page 83)

- pinking shears
- homespun fabric for bag
- embroidery floss
- 1"x20" pinked fabric strip for bow
- photocopy of tag design (page 153) on ecru card stock
- craft glue stick
- green embossed card stock
- decorative-edge craft scissors
- 1/8-inch dia. hole punch
- 1/16-inch dia. gold cord

1. For bag, use pinking shears to cut a 9"x12" piece from homespun. Matching right sides and short edges, fold piece in half. Using a 1/4-inch seam allowance, sew short edges together to form a tube; do not turn right side out.

2. Use floss to baste along bottom edge of tube. Pull threads tight to gather bottom of bag; knot threads to secure…turn bag right side out.

3. Place gift in bag; tie pinked strip into a bow around top of bag.

4. Cut out tag, then glue to card stock. Use craft scissors to trim card stock to 3/8 inch outside edges of design.

5. Punch a hole at top center of tag; use cord to attach tag to knot of bow.

HOUSE APPLIQUÉ BAG

(shown on page 83)

- pinking shears
- fabric for bag
- paper-backed fusible web
- fabric scraps
- black permanent fine-point marker
- recipe card

1. Use pinking shears to cut an 8"x21" piece from fabric for bag. Matching right sides and short edges and using a 1/4-inch seam allowance, sew long edges together for sides of bag.

2. Using patterns, page 157, follow *Making Appliqués*, page 134, to make 3 small window, 2 large window and one each chimney, roof, house, door, wreath and bow appliqués from fabric scraps.

3. Arrange and fuse appliqués on bag. Use marker to draw panes on windows.

4. Write recipe on recipe card. Place gift and recipe card in bag. Tear a 1"x12" strip from fabric scrap; tie strip into a bow around top of bag.

JOLLY GINGERBREAD MEN BASKET

(shown on page 84)

Embellish the handle of a basket with ribbon, greenery and bells…tear a piece of fabric to line the basket. Tuck in the cookie mix, a Gooseberry cookie cutter and a tag made from a photocopy of the recipe on page 156, glued to a piece of brown kraft paper.

131

PATCHWORK POTHOLDER AND TAG

(shown on page 86)

- red fabric scrap for heart
- paper-backed fusible web
- 2 coordinating fabrics for potholder
- polyester bonded batting
- photocopy of tag design (page 156) on brown card stock
- tracing paper
- red embossed card stock
- craft glue stick
- photocopy of instructions (page 156) on tan card stock

1. Using heart pattern, page 156, follow *Making Appliqués*, page 134, to make one heart appliqué from red fabric. Make two 3½-inch square appliqués from one potholder fabric.

2. Cut one 7-inch square from batting and two 7-inch squares from remaining potholder fabric. Arrange and fuse square appliqués, then heart appliqué on right side of one large potholder square. Follow *Machine Appliqué*, page 134, to sew over edges of appliqués.

3. Layer batting between wrong sides of 7-inch squares; baste in place.

4. Piecing as necessary, cut a 2¾"x30" strip from potholder fabric for binding. Press strip in half lengthwise; unfold. Press one long edge ¼ inch to wrong side, then one end ½ inch to wrong side. Beginning with unpressed end, matching raw edges and mitering corners, sew strip along edges on front of potholder.

5. Fold and pin binding to back of potholder, covering basting threads; stitch in place.

6. Cut out tag. Trace heart from tag onto tracing paper and cut out. Use pattern to cut one heart from red card stock...glue over heart on tag. Cut out instructions just outside border...glue to tag.

GENERALS

MAKING A BOW

Loop sizes given in project instructions refer to the length of ribbon used to make one loop of bow.

1. For first streamer, measure desired length of streamer from one end of ribbon; twist ribbon between fingers as shown in Fig. 1.

Fig. 1

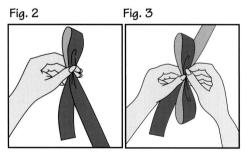

2. Keeping right side of ribbon facing out, fold ribbon to front to form desired-size loop; gather ribbon between fingers (Fig. 2). Fold ribbon to back to form another loop; gather ribbon between fingers (Fig. 3).

Fig. 2   **Fig. 3**

3. If a center loop is desired, form half the desired number of loops, then loosely wrap ribbon around thumb and gather ribbon between fingers as shown in Fig. 4; form

remaining loops. Continue to form loops, varying size of loops as desired, until bow is desired size.

Fig. 4

4. For remaining streamer, trim ribbon to desired length.

5. To secure bow, hold gathered loops tightly. Fold a length of floral wire around gathers of loops. Hold wire ends behind bow, gathering all loops forward; twist bow to tighten wire. Arrange loops and trim ribbon ends as desired.

CROSS STITCH

Preparing floss: If your project will be laundered, soak floss in a mixture of one cup water and one tablespoon vinegar for a few minutes and allow to dry before using to prevent colors from bleeding or fading.

Counted Cross Stitch (X): Work one Cross Stitch to correspond to each colored square in chart. For horizontal rows, work stitches in two journeys (Fig. 1).

Fig. 1

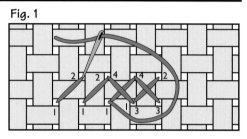

For vertical rows, complete stitch as shown in Fig. 2.

Fig. 2

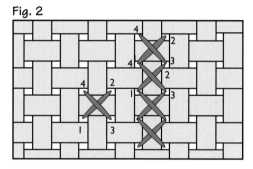

When working over 2 fabric threads, work Cross Stitch as shown.

Backstitch (B'ST): For outline detail, Backstitch (shown in chart and color key by black or colored straight lines) should be worked after all Cross Stitch has been completed.

Fig. 4

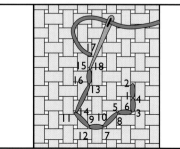

French Knot: Referring to Fig. 5, bring needle up at 1. Wrap floss once around needle and insert needle at 2, holding end of floss with non-stitching fingers.

Fig. 5

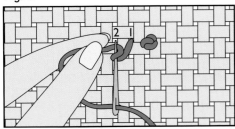

EMBROIDERY STITCHES

Preparing floss: If your project will be laundered, soak floss in a mixture of one cup water and one tablespoon vinegar for a few minutes and allow to dry before using to prevent colors from bleeding or fading.

Backstitch: Referring to Fig. 1, bring needle up at 1; go down at 2; bring up at 3 and pull through. For next stitch, insert needle at 1; bring up at 4 and pull through.

Fig. 1

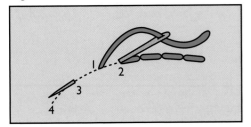

Blanket Stitch: Referring to Fig. 2a, bring needle up at 1. Keeping thread below point of needle, go down at 2 and come up at 3. Continue working as shown in Fig. 2b.

Fig. 2a   **Fig. 2b**

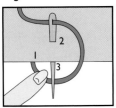
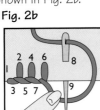

Blind Stitch: Come up at 1. Go down at 2 and come up at 3 (Fig. 3). Length of stitches may be varied as desired.

Fig. 3

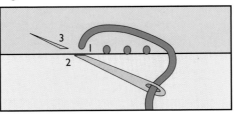

Couched Stitch: Referring to Fig. 4, bring needle up at 1 and go down at 2, following line to be couched. Work tiny stitches over thread to secure.

Fig. 4

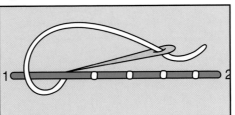

Cross Stitch: Bring needle up at 1 and go down at 2. Come up at 3 and go down at 4 (Fig. 5).

Fig. 5

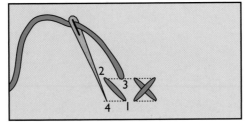

French Knot: Referring to Fig. 6, bring needle up at 1. Wrap floss once around needle and insert needle at 2, holding end of floss with non-stitching fingers. Tighten knot, then pull needle through fabric, holding floss until it must be released. For a larger knot, use more strands; wrap only once.

Fig. 6

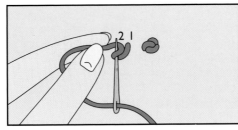

Lazy Daisy Stitch: Bring needle up at 1; take needle down again at 1 to form a loop and bring up at 2. Keeping loop below point of needle (Fig. 7), take needle down at 3 to anchor loop.

Fig. 7

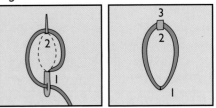

Running Stitch: Referring to Fig. 8, make a series of straight stitches with stitch length equal to the space between stitches.

Fig. 8

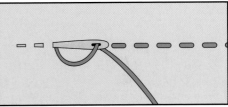

Straight Stitch: Referring to Fig. 9, come up at 1 and go down at 2.

Fig. 9

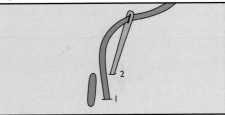

Whip Stitch: Referring to Fig. 10, bring needle up at 1; take thread around edge of fabric and bring needle up at 2. Continue stitching along edge of fabric.

Fig. 10

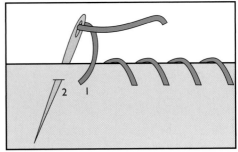

MAKING PATTERNS

When the entire pattern is shown, place tracing paper over the pattern and draw over lines. For a more durable pattern, use a permanent marker to draw over pattern on stencil plastic.

When patterns are stacked or overlapped, place tracing paper over the pattern and follow a single colored line to trace the pattern. Repeat to trace each pattern separately onto tracing paper.

When tracing a two-part pattern, match the dashed lines and arrows to trace an entire pattern onto tracing paper.

When only half of the pattern is shown (indicated by a solid blue line on pattern), fold the tracing paper in half. Place the fold along the solid blue line and trace the pattern half; turn folded paper over and draw over the traced lines on the remaining side. Unfold the pattern; cut out.

MAKING APPLIQUÉS

To prevent darker fabrics from showing through, white or light-colored fabrics may need to be lined with fusible interfacing before being fused.

To make reverse appliqués, trace the pattern onto tracing paper; turn traced paper over and continue to follow all steps using the reversed pattern.

1. Trace the appliqué pattern onto paper side of web as many times as indicated for a single fabric. When making more than one appliqué, leave at least one inch between shapes.

2. Cutting 1/2 inch outside drawn shape, cut out web shape. Fuse to wrong side of fabric.

3. Cut out the appliqué shape along the drawn lines.

MACHINE APPLIQUÉ

Unless otherwise indicated in project instructions, set sewing machine for a medium-width zigzag stitch with a short stitch length. When using nylon or metallic thread, use regular thread in bobbin.

1. Pin or baste a piece of stabilizer slightly larger than design to the wrong side of background fabric under design.

2. Beginning on straight edge of appliqué if possible, position project under presser foot so that most of stitching will be on appliqué piece. Hold upper thread toward you and sew 2 or 3 stitches over thread to prevent raveling. Stitch over all exposed raw edges of appliqué and along detail lines as indicated in project instructions.

3. When stitching is complete, remove stabilizer. Pull loose threads to wrong side of fabric; knot and trim ends.

PAINTING TECHNIQUES

Transferring a pattern: Trace pattern onto tracing paper. Place transfer paper coated-side down between project and traced pattern. Use removable tape to secure pattern to project. Use a pencil to draw over outlines of design (press lightly to avoid smudges and heavy lines that are difficult to cover). If necessary, use a soft eraser to remove any smudges.

Painting basecoats: Use a medium round brush for large areas and a small round brush for small areas. Do not overload brush. Allowing to dry between coats, apply several thin coats of paint to project.

Transferring details: To transfer detail lines to design, reposition pattern and transfer paper over painted basecoats and use a pencil to lightly draw over detail lines of design.

Adding details: Use a permanent marker or paint pen to draw over detail lines.

Sealing: If an item will be handled frequently or used outdoors, we recommend sealing the item with clear acrylic sealer. Sealers are available in spray or brush-on form in several finishes. Follow the manufacturer's instructions to apply the sealer.

Dry Brush: Do not dip brush in water. Dip a stipple brush or old paintbrush in paint; wipe most of the paint off onto a dry paper towel. Lightly rub the brush across the area to receive color. Decrease pressure on the brush as you move outward. Repeat as needed.

Spatter Painting: Dip the bristle tips of a dry toothbrush into paint, blot on a paper towel to remove excess, then pull thumb across bristles to spatter paint on project.

Sponge Painting: Use an assembly-line method when making several sponge-painted projects. Place project on a covered work surface. Practice sponge-painting technique on scrap paper until desired look is achieved. Paint projects with first color and allow to dry before moving to next color. Use a clean sponge for each additional color.

For allover designs, dip a dampened sponge piece into paint; remove excess paint on a paper towel. Use a light stamping motion to paint item.

For painting with sponge shapes, dip a dampened sponge shape into paint; remove excess paint on a paper towel. Lightly press sponge shape onto project. Carefully lift sponge. For a reverse design, turn sponge shape over.

STENCILING

These instructions are written for multicolor stencils. For single-color stencils, make one stencil for entire design.

1. For first stencil, cut a piece from stencil plastic one inch larger than entire pattern. Center plastic over pattern and use a permanent pen to trace outlines of all areas of first color in stencil cutting key. For placement guidelines, outline remaining colored area using dashed lines. Using a new piece of plastic for each additional color in stencil cutting key, repeat for remaining stencils.

2. Place each plastic piece on cutting mat and use craft knife to cut out stencil along solid lines, making sure edges are smooth.

3. Hold or tape stencil in place. Using a clean, dry stencil brush or sponge piece, dip brush or sponge in paint. Remove excess paint on a paper towel. Brush or sponge should be almost dry to produce best results. Beginning at edge of cut-out area, apply paint in a stamping motion over stencil. If desired, highlight or shade design by stamping a lighter or darker shade of paint in cut-out area. Repeat until all areas of first stencil have been painted. Carefully remove stencil and allow paint to dry.

4. Using stencils in order indicated in color key and matching guidelines on stencils to previously stenciled area, repeat Step 3 for remaining stencils.

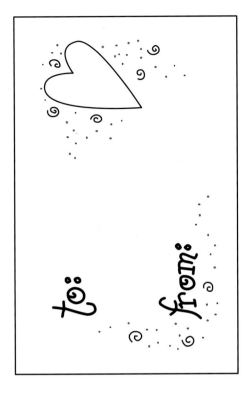

Gooseberry Patch and Leisure Arts, Inc.,
grant permission to the owner of this
book to photocopy the tags on this
page for personal use only.

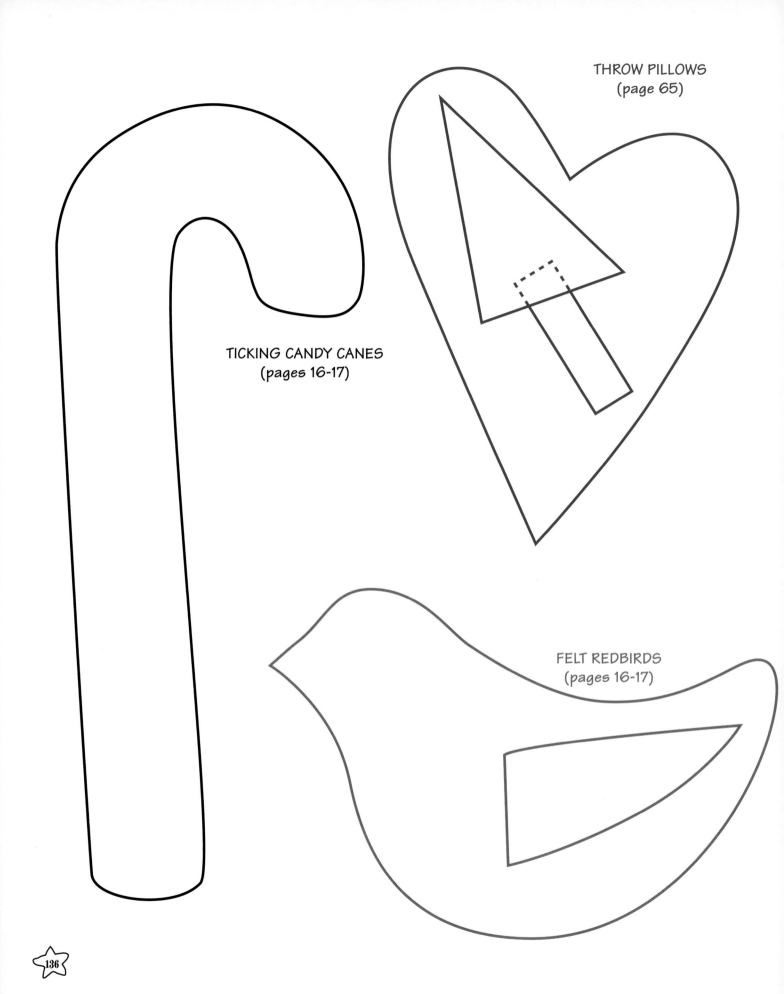

THROW PILLOWS
(page 65)

TICKING CANDY CANES
(pages 16-17)

FELT REDBIRDS
(pages 16-17)

KID'S CHRISTMAS CARD KIT
(page 66)

COPPER-TOP GIFT BOXES
(page 57)

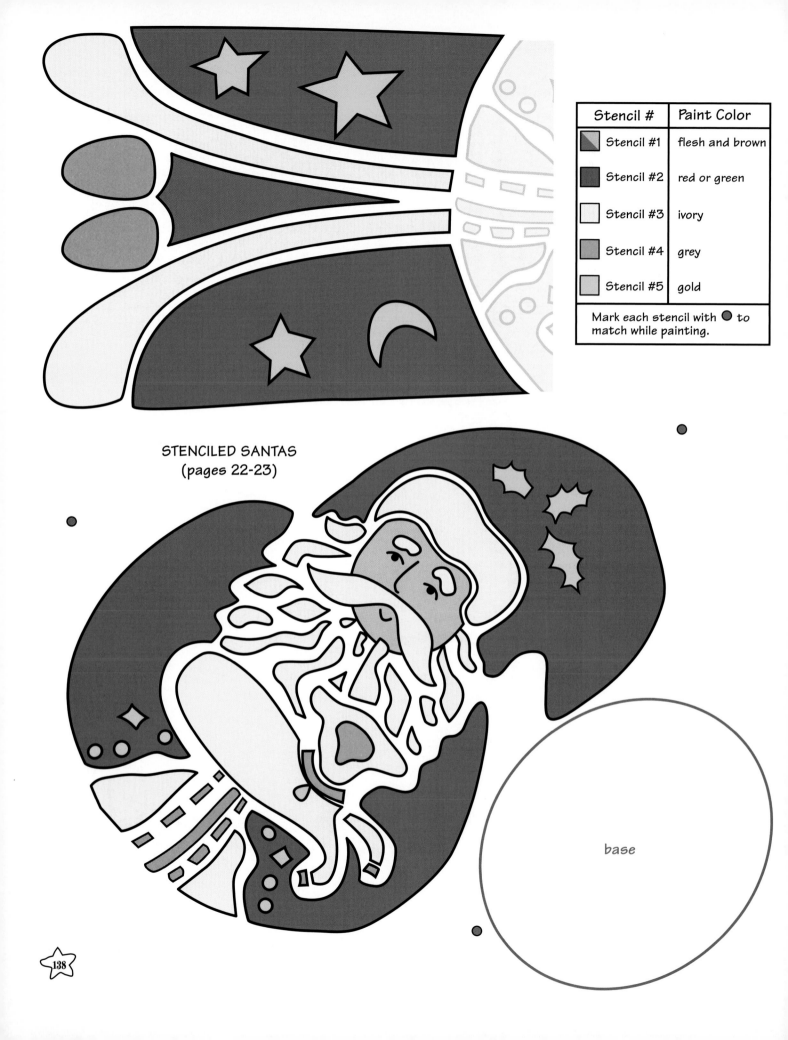

Stencil #	Paint Color
Stencil #1	flesh and brown
Stencil #2	red or green
Stencil #3	ivory
Stencil #4	grey
Stencil #5	gold
Mark each stencil with ● to match while painting.	

STENCILED SANTAS
(pages 22-23)

base

WARM THOUGHTS JAR
(page 29)

Warm thoughts

Gooseberry Patch and Leisure Arts, Inc., grant permission to the owner of this book to photocopy the designs on this page for personal use only.

CHICKEN FEEDER CANDLEHOLDER
(page 51)

PATCHWORK POTHOLDER
AND TAG
(page 86)

EMBROIDERED
MUSLIN STOCKING
(page 34)

Red
Brown
Gold
Peach
Black
Winter White
Blue
Green
Beige Heather

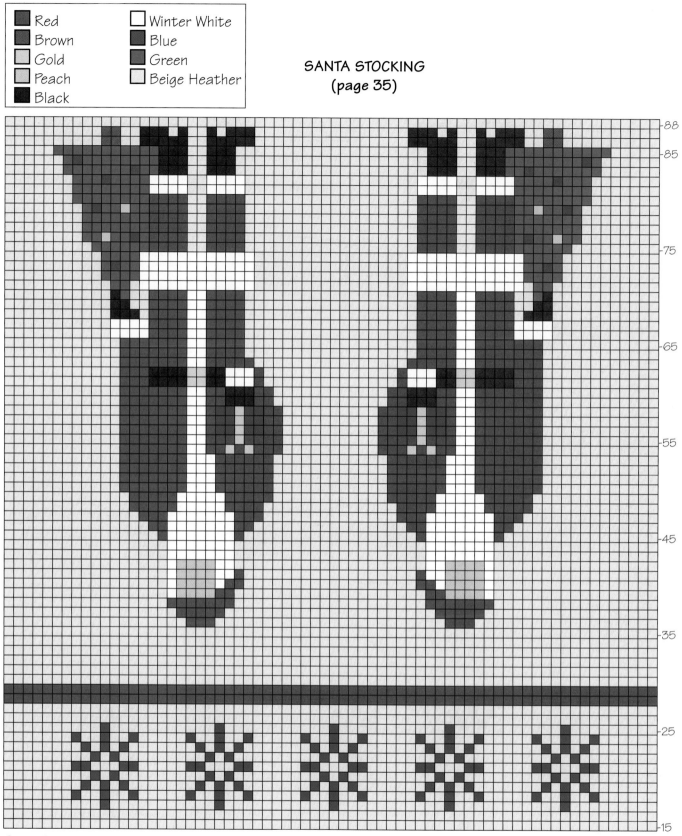

On **right** side rows, work chart from **right** to **left**; on **wrong** side rows, work chart from **left** to **right**.

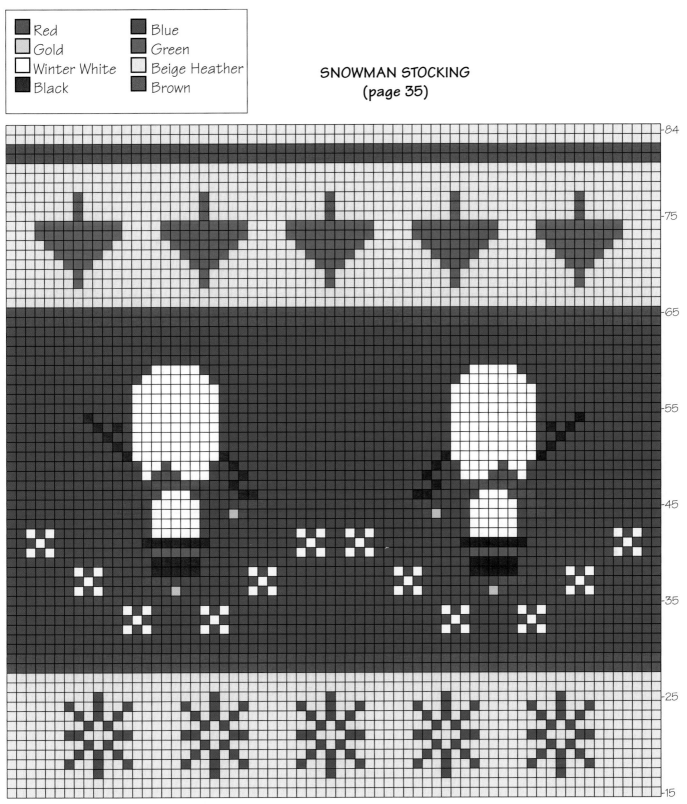

Red
Gold
Winter White
Black
Blue
Green
Beige Heather
Brown

SNOWMAN STOCKING
(page 35)

On **right** side rows, work chart from **right** to **left**; on **wrong** side rows, work chart from **left** to **right**.

141

Welcome Home

"WELCOME HOME" DOOR PILLOW
(page 18)

TICKING TREE
(page 40)

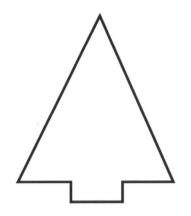

BUTTON-RIMMED BASKET
(pages 74-75)

PLAY DOUGH JARS
(page 68)

Gooseberry Patch and Leisure Arts, Inc., grant permission to the owner of this book to photocopy the designs on this page for personal use only.

TICKING TREE
(page 40)

Sparkles & wishes

hopes & dreams

SNACK BAG
(pages 74-75)

143

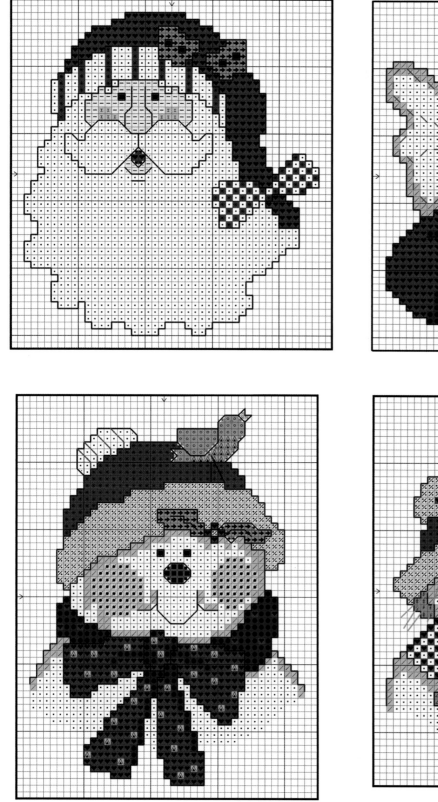

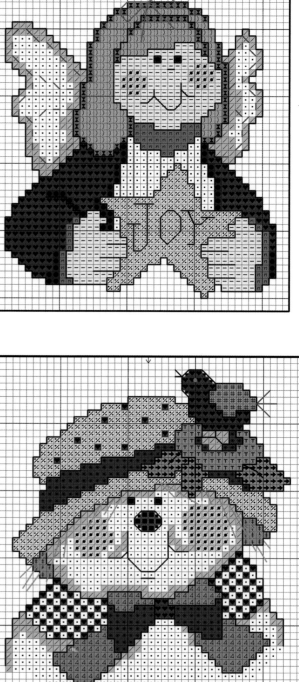

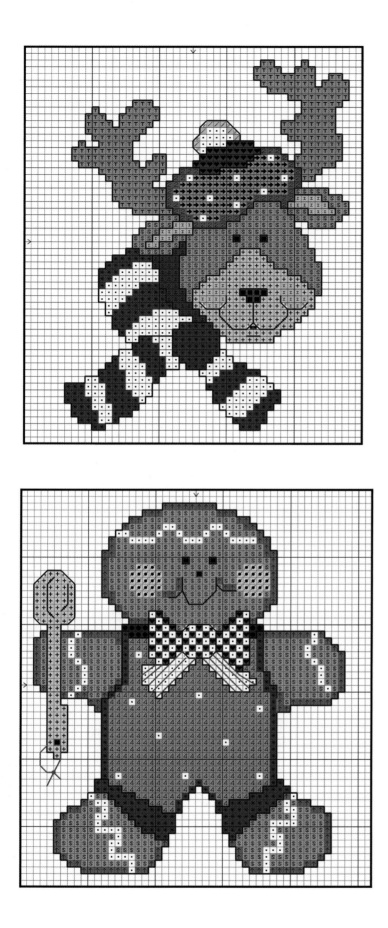

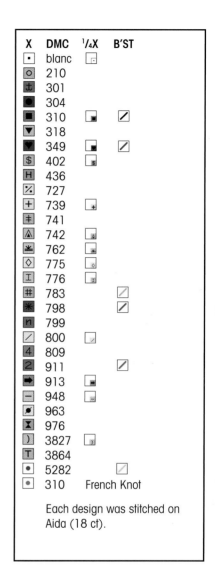

X	DMC	¼X	B'ST
·	blanc	·	
o	210		
⊞	301		
●	304		
■	310	■	╱
▼	318		
▼	349	▼	╱
$	402	s	
H	436		
%	727		
+	739	+	
‡	741		
▲	742	▲	
※	762	※	
◇	775	◇	
Ⅰ	776	Ⅰ	
#	783		╱
✳	798		╱
₪	799		
╱	800	╱	
4	809		
2	911		╱
➡	913	➡	
−	948	−	
◢	963		
✕	976		
)	3827	)	
T	3864		
•	5282		╱
•	310	French Knot	

Each design was stitched on
Aida (18 ct).

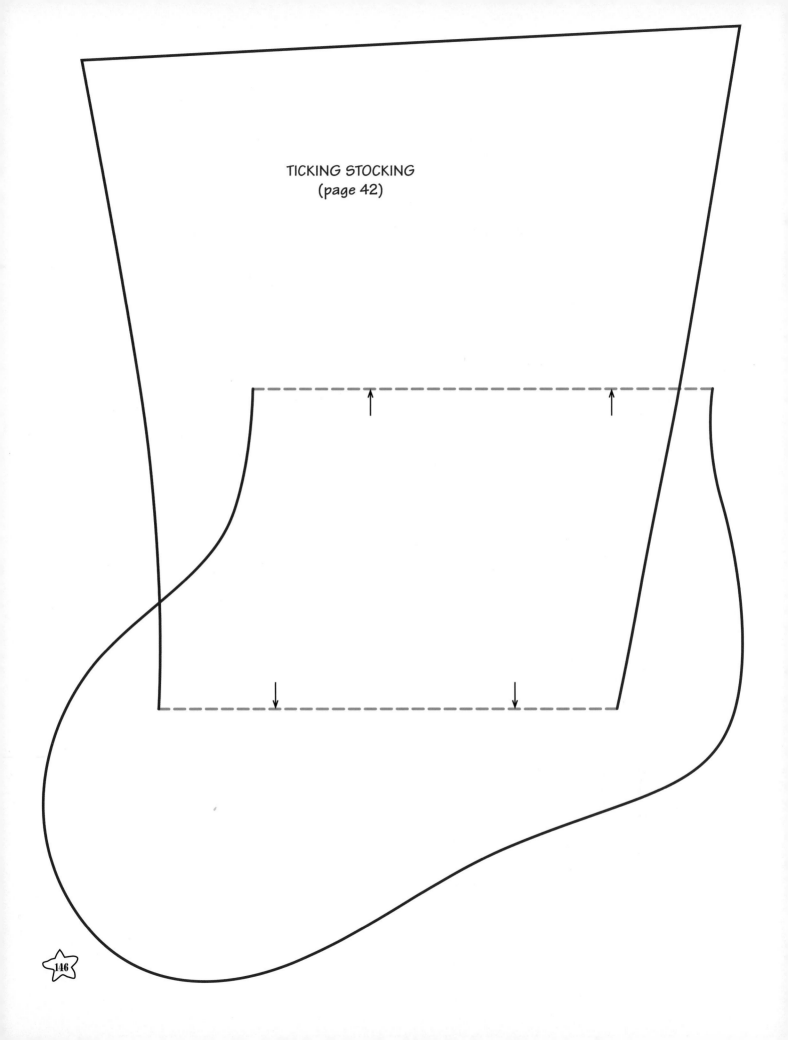

TICKING STOCKING
(page 42)

Christmas comes but once a year....

Christmas comes but once a year....

COPPER-TOP GIFT BOXES
(page 57)

FRAMED AND WINDOW SNOWFLAKES
(pages 20-21)

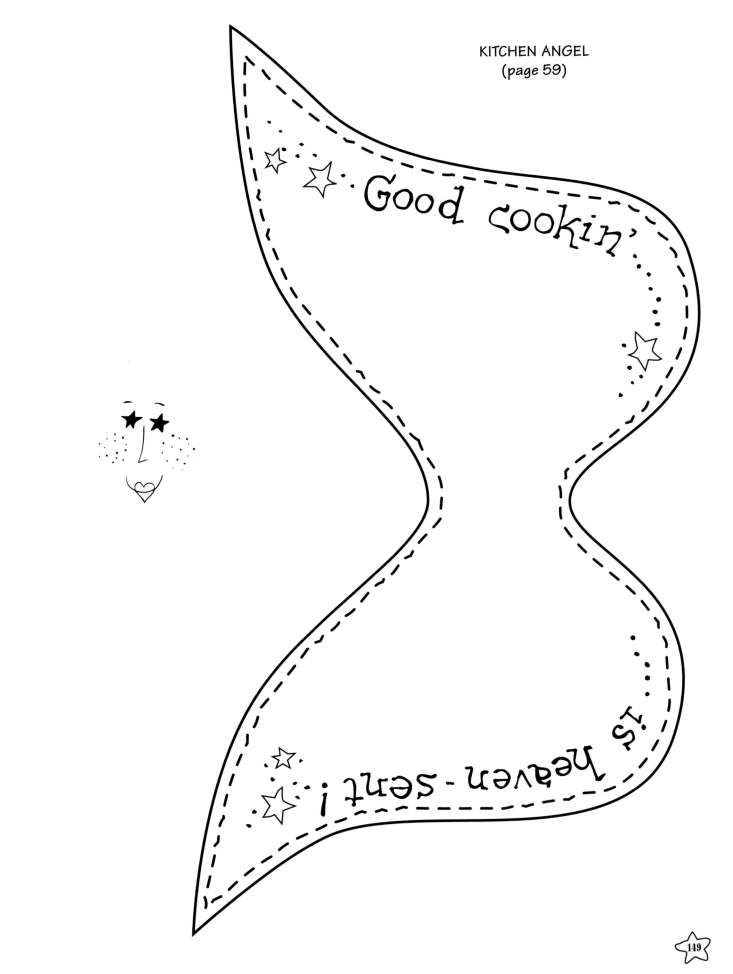

Good cookin'... is heaven-sent!

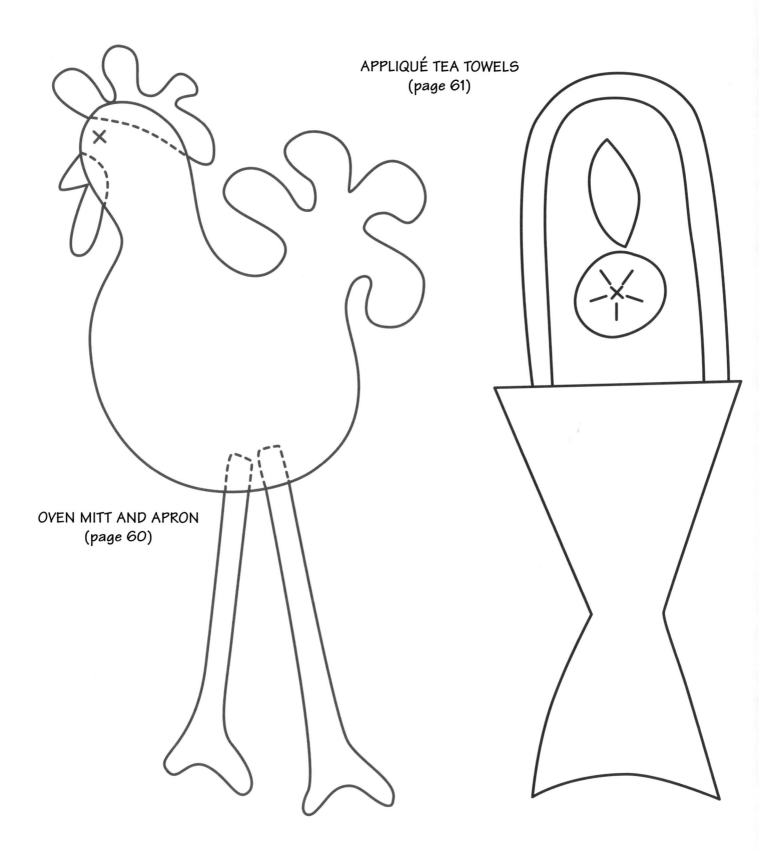

APPLIQUÉ TEA TOWELS
(page 61)

OVEN MITT AND APRON
(page 60)

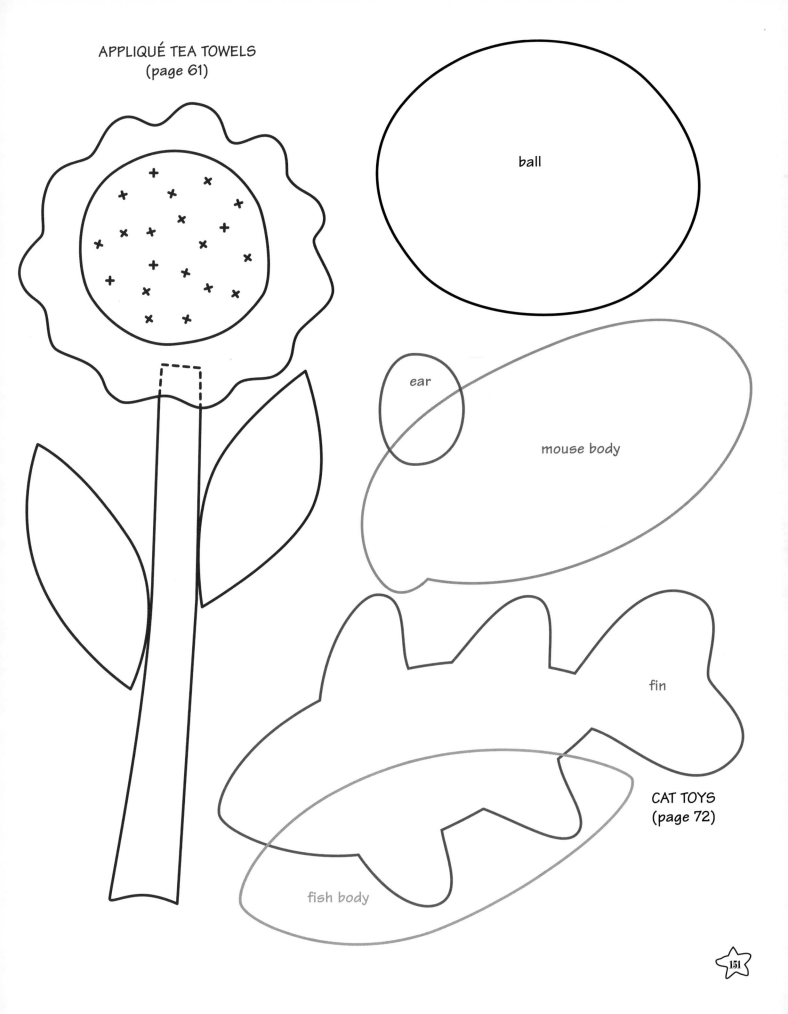

APPLIQUÉ TEA TOWELS
(page 61)

ball

ear

mouse body

fin

fish body

CAT TOYS
(page 72)

151

PRIMITIVE EMBROIDERED SWEATER
(page 62)

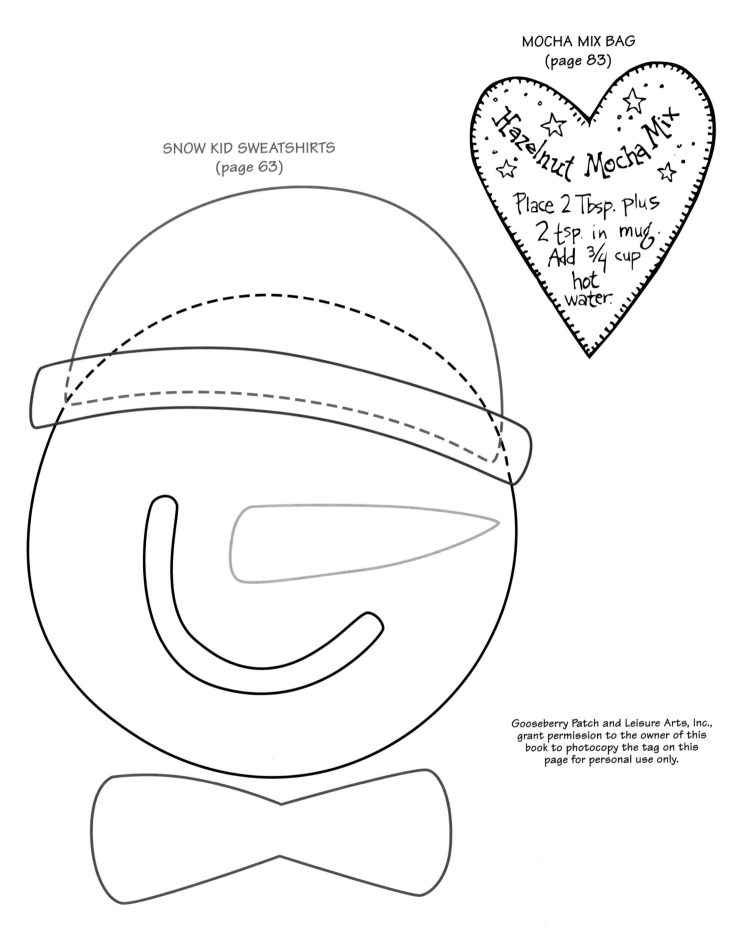

SNOW KID SWEATSHIRTS
(page 63)

MOCHA MIX BAG
(page 83)

Hazelnut Mocha Mix

Place 2 Tbsp. plus 2 tsp. in mug. Add ¾ cup hot water.

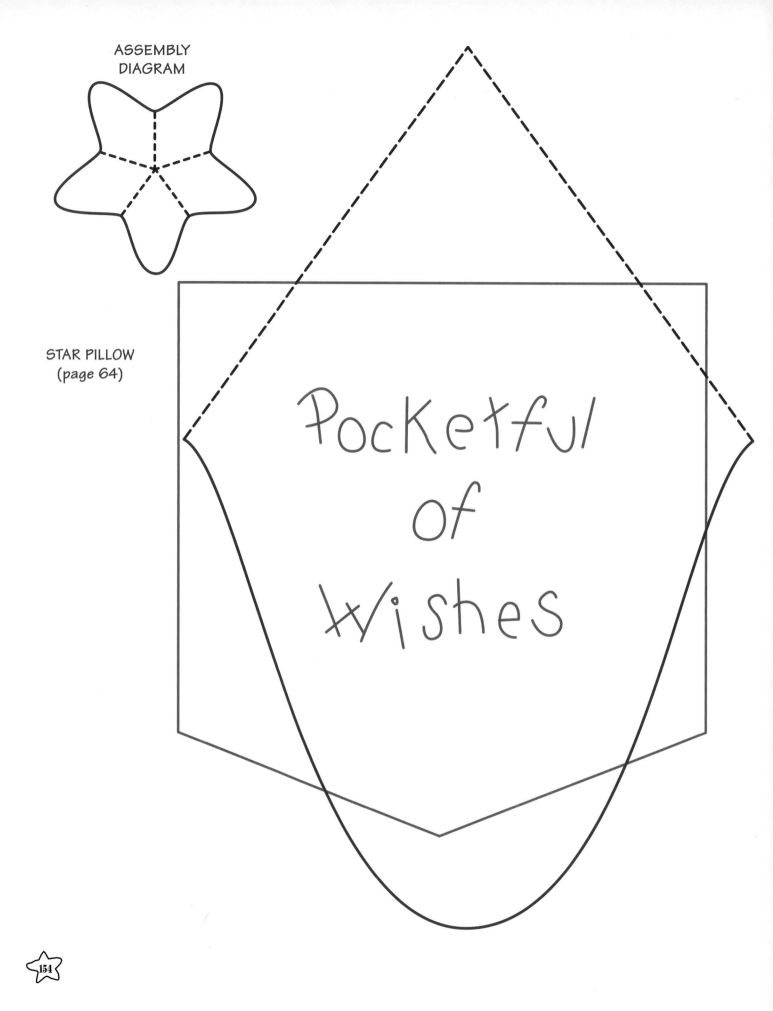

ASSEMBLY
DIAGRAM

STAR PILLOW
(page 64)

Pocketful
of
Wishes

PATCHWORK POTHOLDER AND TAG
(page 86)

JOLLY GINGERBREAD MEN MIX
(page 84)

Cream together ¹/₂ cup butter, ³/₄ cup molasses and one egg; stir in dry mix. Dough will be stiff. Cover and refrigerate one hour. Roll dough to ¹/₄-inch thickness on a lightly floured surface; add additional flour if dough is too sticky. Cut with a 4¹/₄"x3¹/₂" gingerbread boy cookie cutter and place on a lightly greased baking sheet. Bake at 350 degrees for 10 to 12 minutes. Makes about 22 cookies.

Add beans to a large stockpot; cover with hot water and let soak overnight. Drain and add 2 quarts of water. Bring to a boil; reduce heat and simmer, covered, one to 2 hours or until beans are almost tender. Stir in two 14¹/₂-ounce cans stewed tomatoes and seasoning mix. Simmer, uncovered, one to 1¹/₂ hours or until beans are tender. Makes approximately 12 cups of soup.

PANCAKES FROM THE PANTRY
(page 81)

In a large mixing bowl, add 2 eggs; beat well. Gradually beat in ¹/₃ cup oil. Alternately add 2 cups of pancake mix and 1 cup of water to the egg mixture; blend well. Cook pancakes on a lightly oiled griddle. Makes 10 pancakes.

PINE CONE FIRESTARTERS
(page 52)

WINTERTIME SPICE TEA CUP
(page 81)

WINTERTIME SPICE TEA

Add 3 to 4 teaspoons to one cup of hot water, stir well.

CRANBERRY BREAD BAG
(page 77)

Cranberry Bread

CINNAMON CRUNCH BASKET
(pages 74-75)

Cinnamon Crunch Bars

HOUSE APPLIQUÉ BAG
(page 83)

PROJECT INDEX

RECIPE INDEX

Credits

We want to extend a warm *thank you* to the people who allowed us to photograph our projects at their homes: Carl and Monte Brunck, Tommy and Donna Harkins, Charles and Peg Mills, and Duncan and Nancy Porter.

We want to especially thank photographers Andy Uilkie and Ken West of Peerless Photography, Jerry R. Davis of Jerry Davis Photography, and Nancy Nolan of Nola Studios, all of Little Rock, Arkansas, for their excellent work. Photography stylist Jan Nobles also deserves a special mention for the high quality of her collaboration with these photographers.

To Wisconsin Technicolor LLC, of Pewaukee, Wisconsin, we say *thank you* for the superb color reproduction and excellent pre-press preparation.

We extend a special word of thanks to Linda Gillum of Kooler Design Studio, who created the Cross-Stitched Ornaments on pages 44-45.

Thanks also go to Kathleen Royal Phillips, who assisted Oxmoor House with some of the recipes in this book.

Hmmmmmmm....

THe Healthful Hunger for A **great idea** is the beauty and blessedness of life.

— JEAN INGELOW —